THE LADYBIRD PICTURE ATLAS

Continents and Oceans

Round maps like the ones below show what the Earth looks like from space. The Earth is almost a sphere, but it is flattened at the Poles and it bulges in the middle. It is divided into two halves, called *hemispheres* (half spheres), by an imaginary line around the middle. This line is called the *equator*. Other imaginary lines around the Earth are also shown in red on the maps.

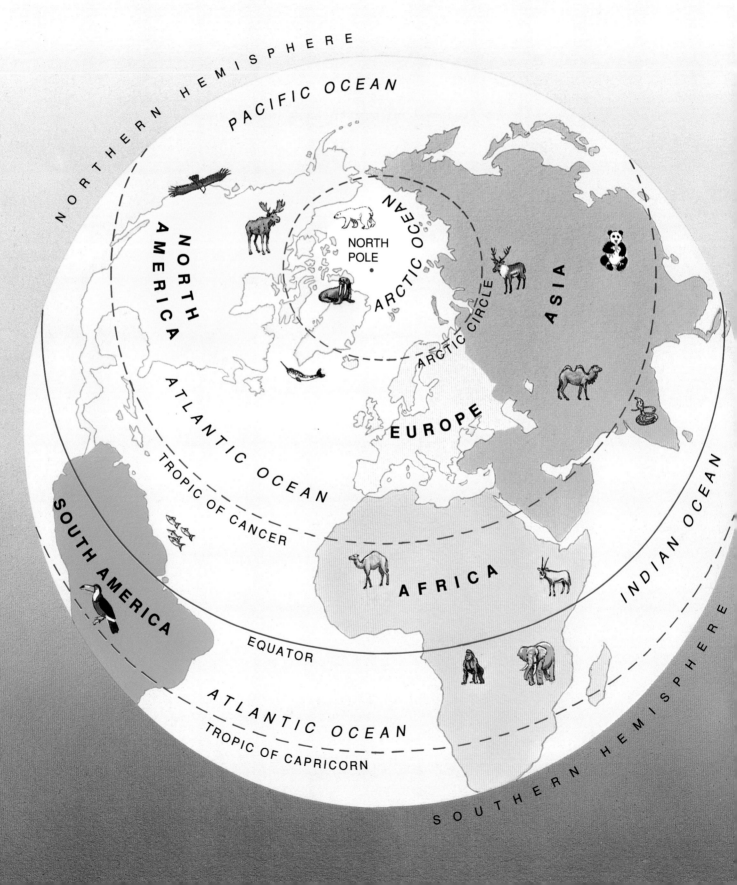

The land is divided into seven areas called *continents*. Asia is the biggest continent and Australasia is the smallest. The oceans cover more than two thirds of the Earth. The Pacific is the largest ocean, and the smallest is the Arctic Ocean. As you can see, the southern hemisphere has far more water than the northern.

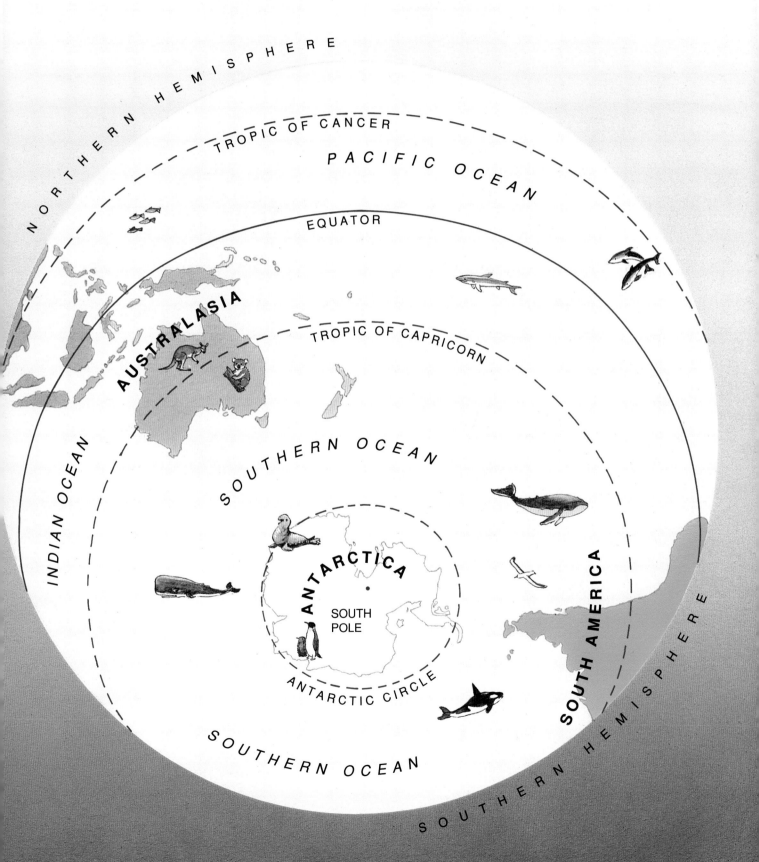

About this Atlas

Today everyone is used to seeing and hearing news and stories from every part of the world. But you may not be quite sure exactly where the places that you hear about are to be found. In this *Ladybird Picture Atlas* you will find maps full of information about the world we live in. Colourful symbols and illustrations show you at a glance the main features of each country. Fact boxes and an index of over 1,000 places help you to find out more. By using *The Ladybird Picture Atlas,* you will discover how maps work and enjoy developing the skills that will increase your knowledge and understanding of our world.

Designers: John Dillow, Philip Leafe, Roy Smith
Editors: Stephanie Barton, Nicola Baxter,
             Marie Birkinshaw, Catriona Macgregor,
             Ronne Randall
Geography Consultant: Don Longworth
Educational Consultant: Geraldine Taylor

Acknowledgments
Many people have been involved in the planning and preparation of this Atlas. They include editors, advisers, embassies, regional and cultural specialists worldwide, linguists, and those who have supplied technical support and advice. To all who have contributed in any way, the publishers wish to extend their sincere thanks.

The publishers have made every effort to ensure that the maps and information in this Atlas are correct at time of publishing. There is however no intended implication that the publishers necessarily endorse or accept the status of any political entity recorded in this book.

Ladybird books are widely available, but in case of difficulty may be ordered by post or telephone from:
Ladybird Books – Cash Sales Department Littlegate Road Paignton Devon TQ3 3BE Telephone 01803 554761

A catalogue record for this book is available from the British Library

Published by Ladybird Books Ltd Loughborough Leicestershire UK
Ladybird Books Inc Auburn Maine 04210 USA

Typesetting by Oxford Cartographers

PICTURE ATLAS

illustrations by John Dillow
text by Anita Ganeri

Contents

How to use this Atlas

This is a book of maps of the countries of the world. Maps can show the shapes and features of countries much smaller than in real life. The world is round but most maps are flat. To make the surface of the world seem flat, map-makers have to divide it into segments rather like peeling an orange.

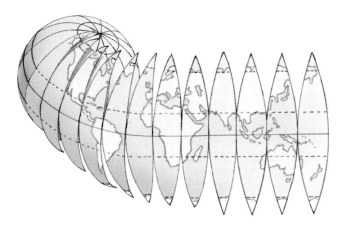

We have used this kind of flattened out map on the main maps to show you where a country or continent is in the world.

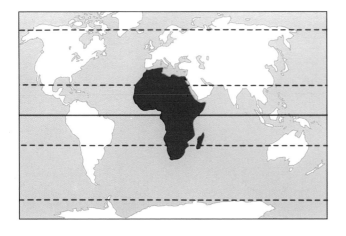

Of course, the maps in this book show things much smaller than they really are. The scale helps you to work out how much smaller the map is. Scales in this book are written like this ▶

Sometimes it is not possible to fit all of one map on to the page. If a piece of land has been moved from its real position, it will have a box round it as below. It may not be to the same scale as the rest of the map.

THE FAEROES

NORWEGIAN SEA

Maps also show the names of places. Different people may call the same place by a different name. If there are two common ways of naming a place, both are given on the map, for example: Beijing (Peking).
The way that the name is printed can give you other clues about what you see.

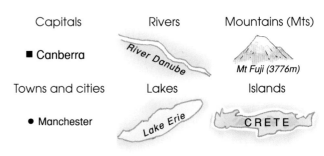

Capitals	Rivers	Mountains (Mts)
■ Canberra	River Danube	Mt Fuji (3776m)
Towns and cities	Lakes	Islands
● Manchester	Lake Erie	CRETE

10 mm on the map is really a distance of about **140 km (87 miles)**

Symbols

On the maps there are many small pictures to give you more information about the countries shown. Most of these are symbols that appear many times and have a special meaning.

 temperate fruit (not tropical)

 industry

 citrus fruit

 minerals

 tropical fruit

 coal mines

 grapes

 gold

 groundnuts (peanuts)

 diamonds

 olives

 oil wells

 dates

 gas or oil at sea

 rubber

 timber

 tobacco

 geysers

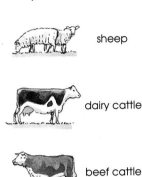 sheep

 silk

 dairy cattle

 tea

 beef cattle

 cocoa

 pigs

 coffee

 sugar beet

 rice

 sugar cane

 cereal crops

 cotton

 maize

 fishing

 tourism

Endangered species

The changes that human beings have made to the world have meant that many animals are now endangered. Some of these are shown on the maps in a red circle. Can you find these animals?

 giant panda

 gorilla

 red ruffed lemur

 jaguar

 African elephant

 blue whale

 black rhino

white whale

 Arabian oryx

 Javan rhino

orang -utan

Bengal tiger

The World

The world is divided into over 160 countries.
A country usually has its own leaders and
makes its own laws.

Can you find your own country on this map?

ARCTIC OCEAN

GREENLAND
(DENMARK)

ARCTIC CIRCLE

ALASKA
(USA)

ICELAND

CANADA

UNITED
KINGDOM

REPUBLIC OF IRELAND

UNITED STATES
OF AMERICA

ATLANTIC
OCEAN

SPAIN

PORTUGAL

MEXICO

BERMUDA

MOROCCO

TROPIC OF CANCER

BAHAMAS

WESTERN
SAHARA

ALG

CUBA

HAWAII
(USA)

CAYMAN
ISLANDS

HAITI

DOMINICAN REPUBLIC
PUERTO RICO (USA)
ANTIGUA & BARBUDA
DOMINICA

CAPE VERDE
ISLANDS

MAURITANIA

MA

BELIZE

JAMAICA

ST KITTS & NEVIS

ST LUCIA
BARBADOS

SENEGAL

GAMBIA

GUINEA-BISSAU

BURKINA
FASO

GUATEMALA
EL SALVADOR

HONDURAS

NICARAGUA

GRENADA

ST VINCENT & THE GRENADINES
TRINIDAD & TOBAGO

GUINEA

GHANA

PACIFIC
OCEAN

COSTA RICA

PANAMA

VENEZUELA

GUYANA

SURINAME

SIERRA LEONE

IVORY
COAST

LIBERIA

COLOMBIA

FRENCH GUIANA

TOGO

EQUATOR

ECUADOR

GALAPAGOS
ISLANDS
(ECUADOR)

SAO

WESTERN
SAMOA

MARQUESAS
(FRANCE)

PERU

BRAZIL

TONGA

SOCIETY
ISLANDS
(FRANCE)

COOK
ISLANDS (NZ)

BOLIVIA

TROPIC OF CAPRICORN

PARAGUAY

The names of the countries that are
numbered on the map are:

ATLANTIC
OCEAN

I ESTONIA	13 LUXEMBOURG
2 LATVIA	14 LIECHTENSTEIN
3 LITHUANIA	15 SWITZERLAND
4 BELARUS	16 CZECH REPUBLIC
5 GEORGIA	17 SLOVAK REPUBLIC
6 ARMENIA	18 AUSTRIA
7 AZERBAIJAN	19 HUNGARY
8 TADJIKISTAN	20 MOLDOVA
9 KYRGYZSTAN	21 ROMANIA
10 DENMARK	22 BULGARIA
11 NETHERLANDS	23 ALBANIA
12 BELGIUM	24 ANDORRA
	25 YUGOSLAVIA including
	SLOVENIA
	CROATIA

CHILE

ARGENTINA

URUGUAY

FALKLAND
ISLANDS (UK)

ANTARCTIC CIRCLE

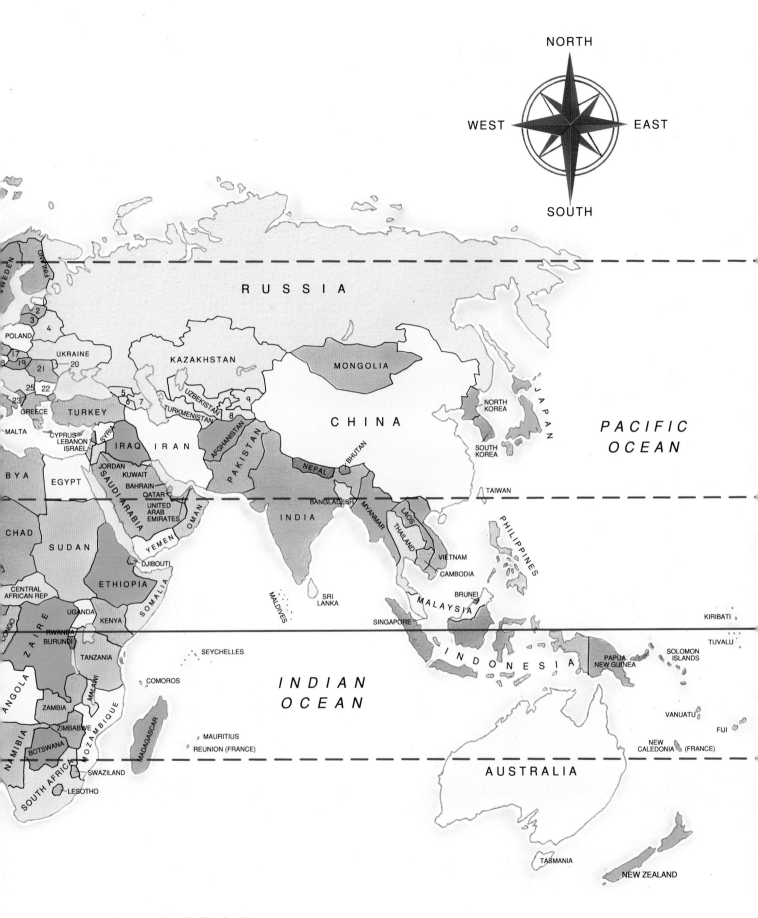

NORTH

WEST

EAST

SOUTH

RUSSIA

SWEDEN

FINLAND

2

3

4

POLAND

17

19

21

20

UKRAINE

25

22

23

GREECE

KAZAKHSTAN

MONGOLIA

5

6

7

UZBEKISTAN

9

8

TURKMENISTAN

TURKEY

MALTA

CYPRUS
LEBANON
ISRAEL

SYRIA

IRAQ

IRAN

AFGHANISTAN

PAKISTAN

CHINA

NORTH
KOREA

SOUTH
KOREA

JAPAN

PACIFIC
OCEAN

BYA

EGYPT

JORDAN

KUWAIT

BAHRAIN

QATAR

UNITED
ARAB
EMIRATES

SAUDI ARABIA

OMAN

NEPAL

BHUTAN

TAIWAN

CHAD

SUDAN

YEMEN

DJIBOUTI

BANGLADESH

INDIA

MYANMAR

LAOS

THAILAND

VIETNAM

CAMBODIA

PHILIPPINES

CENTRAL
AFRICAN REP

ETHIOPIA

SOMALIA

MALDIVES

SRI
LANKA

BRUNEI

MALAYSIA

KIRIBATI

CONGO

UGANDA

KENYA

SINGAPORE

TUVALU

ZAIRE

RWANDA
BURUNDI

TANZANIA

SEYCHELLES

INDONESIA

PAPUA
NEW GUINEA

SOLOMON
ISLANDS

ANGOLA

ZAMBIA

MALAWI

COMOROS

INDIAN
OCEAN

VANUATU

FIJI

NAMIBIA

ZIMBABWE

BOTSWANA

MOZAMBIQUE

MADAGASCAR

MAURITIUS

REUNION (FRANCE)

NEW
CALEDONIA (FRANCE)

SOUTH AFRICA

SWAZILAND

LESOTHO

AUSTRALIA

TASMANIA

NEW ZEALAND

OUTHERN OCEAN

TARCTICA

World Environments

This map shows some of the different natural environments in the world. Your environment is the area around you, including all the living and non-living things in it. Every environment has its own features, such as climate, plants and animals, rivers and mountains.

Many plants and animals have special characteristics that help them survive in their environment. The polar bear's thick coat, for example, keeps it warm in icy temperatures. The environment also affects how people live.

ARCTIC OCEAN

PACIFIC OCEAN

NORTH AMERICA

ATLANTIC OCEAN

SOUTH AMERICA

GRASSLAND
Grasslands are found in hot and cold countries and always have a wet and dry season. The main plants are tough, short grasses and herbs.

SAVANNA
These are grasslands found in hot, tropical areas. They have a rainy season followed by a dry one.

MEDITERRANEAN WOODLAND SCRUB
These places have hot, dry summers and mild winters. Olive trees are common.

DESERT
Deserts are the hottest, driest places on Earth, with less than 100 mm of rain a year.

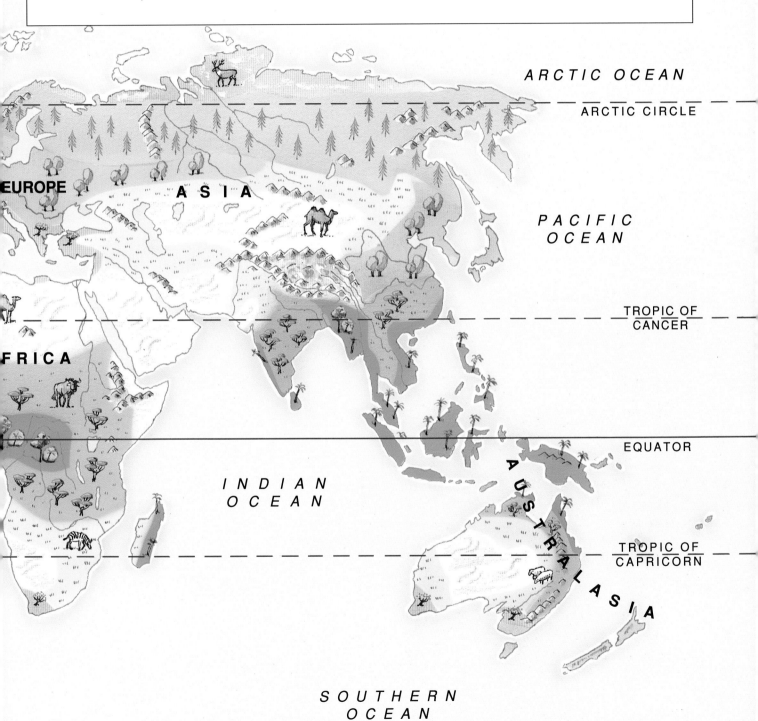

POLAR
The Poles are windswept and icy all year round. In winter, days may be as dark as nights.

MOUNTAINOUS
Mountains get colder as you go higher. Different kinds of plants and animals can live at different levels.

BROADLEAVED FOREST
Broadleaved forests grow in mild areas. Trees include beech, oak and ash.

TUNDRA
In summer, the snow on the tundra melts but the ground below stays frozen. It is called permafrost.

CONIFEROUS FOREST
This band of forest contains trees that can survive the cold. They include pine, spruce and larch.

TROPICAL RAINFOREST
These jungles are hot and wet all year round. They are very rich in wildlife.

ARCTIC OCEAN

ARCTIC CIRCLE

EUROPE

ASIA

PACIFIC OCEAN

TROPIC OF CANCER

FRICA

EQUATOR

INDIAN OCEAN

AUSTRALASIA

TROPIC OF CAPRICORN

SOUTHERN OCEAN

ANTARCTIC CIRCLE

ANTARCTICA

The British Isles

The British Isles are made up of two large islands and many smaller ones. The islands are divided into two countries – the United Kingdom and the Republic of Ireland.

The United Kingdom is made up of Scotland, England, Wales and Northern Ireland. The British Isles have many factories and industries, but farming is also important.

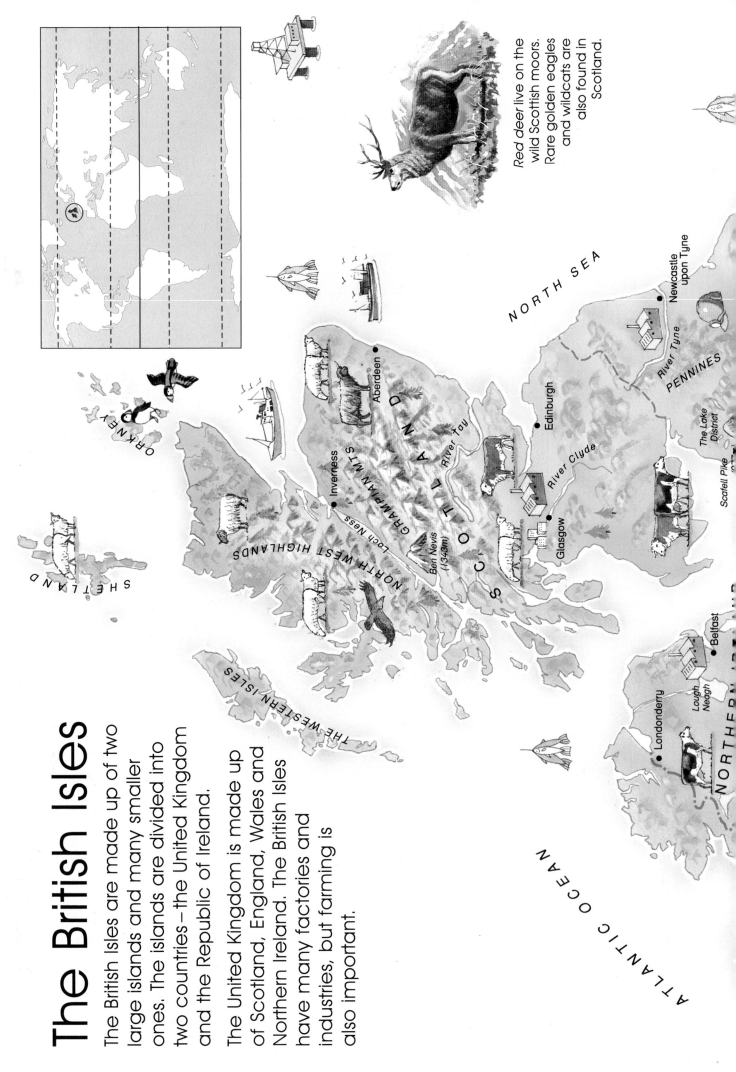

Red deer live on the wild Scottish moors. Rare golden eagles and wildcats are also found in Scotland.

SHETLAND

ORKNEY

THE WESTERN ISLES

NORTH WEST HIGHLANDS

Loch Ness

GRAMPIAN MTS

Inverness

Aberdeen

GRANDTIANS

Ben Nevis
(1343m)

River Tay

S C O T L A N D

Glasgow

River Clyde

Edinburgh

PENNINES

River Tyne

Newcastle upon Tyne

NORTH SEA

The Lake District

Scafell Pike

NORTHERN IRELAND

Belfast

Lough Neagh

Londonderry

ATLANTIC OCEAN

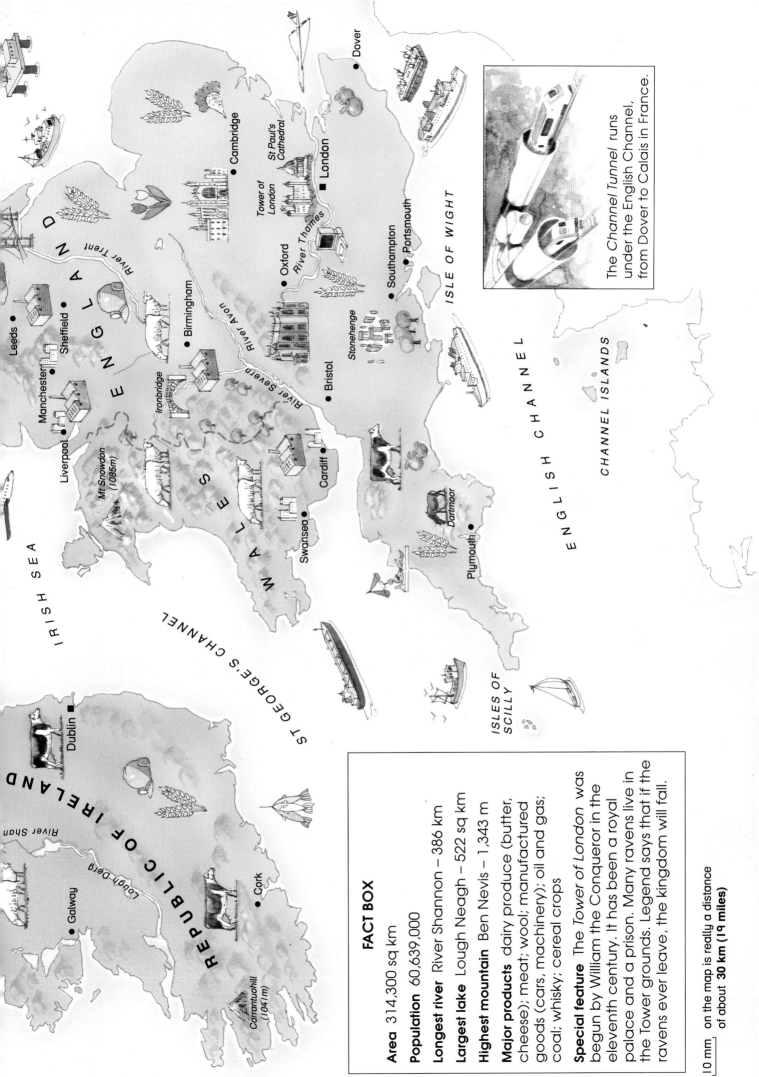

FACT BOX

Area 314,300 sq km

Population 60,639,000

Longest river River Shannon – 386 km

Largest lake Lough Neagh – 522 sq km

Highest mountain Ben Nevis – 1,343 m

Major products dairy produce (butter, cheese); meat; wool; manufactured goods (cars, machinery); oil and gas; coal; whisky; cereal crops

Special feature The *Tower of London* was begun by William the Conqueror in the eleventh century. It has been a royal palace and a prison. Many ravens live in the Tower grounds. Legend says that if the ravens ever leave, the kingdom will fall.

The *Channel Tunnel* runs under the English Channel, from Dover to Calais in France.

10 mm on the map is really a distance of about **30 km (19 miles)**

Northern Europe

This part of Europe is made up of five countries – Iceland, Finland, Norway, Sweden and Denmark. Denmark is low-lying but much of Norway and Sweden is mountainous. There are also lakes and forests throughout the region, and even volcanoes in Iceland.

People called *Lapps* live in the far north of Norway, Sweden and Finland, above the Arctic Circle. This region is called Lapland. Many Lapps are reindeer herders.

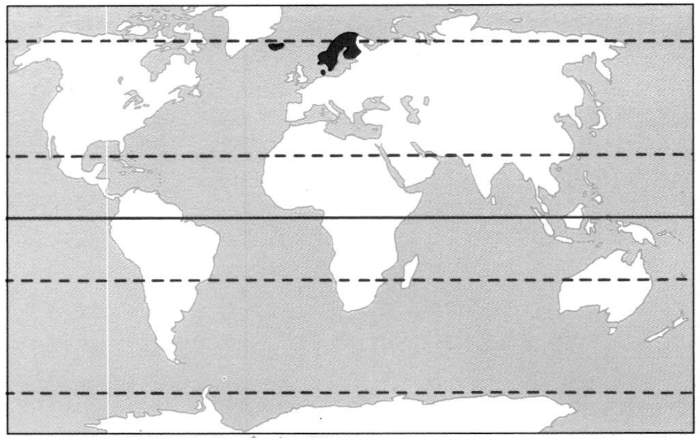

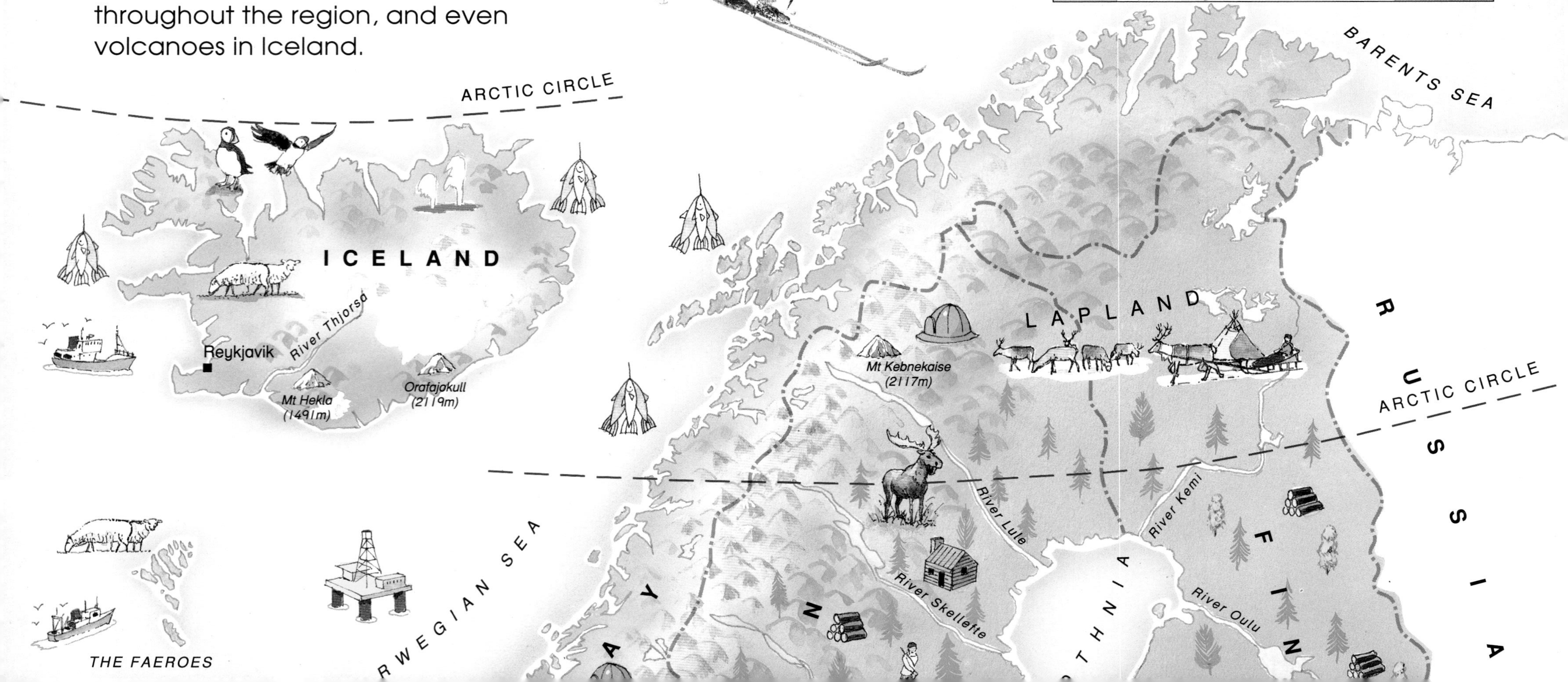

BARENTS SEA

R U S S I A

ARCTIC CIRCLE

F I N

River Oulu

River Kemi

L A P L A N D

River Lule

N I H T O B

Mt Kebnekaise
(2117m)

River Skellefte

N

N O R W E G I A N S E A

Y A W R O N

ARCTIC CIRCLE

I C E L A N D

Öraefajökull
(2119m)

River Thjorsa

Reykjavik

Mt Hekla
(1491m)

THE FAEROES

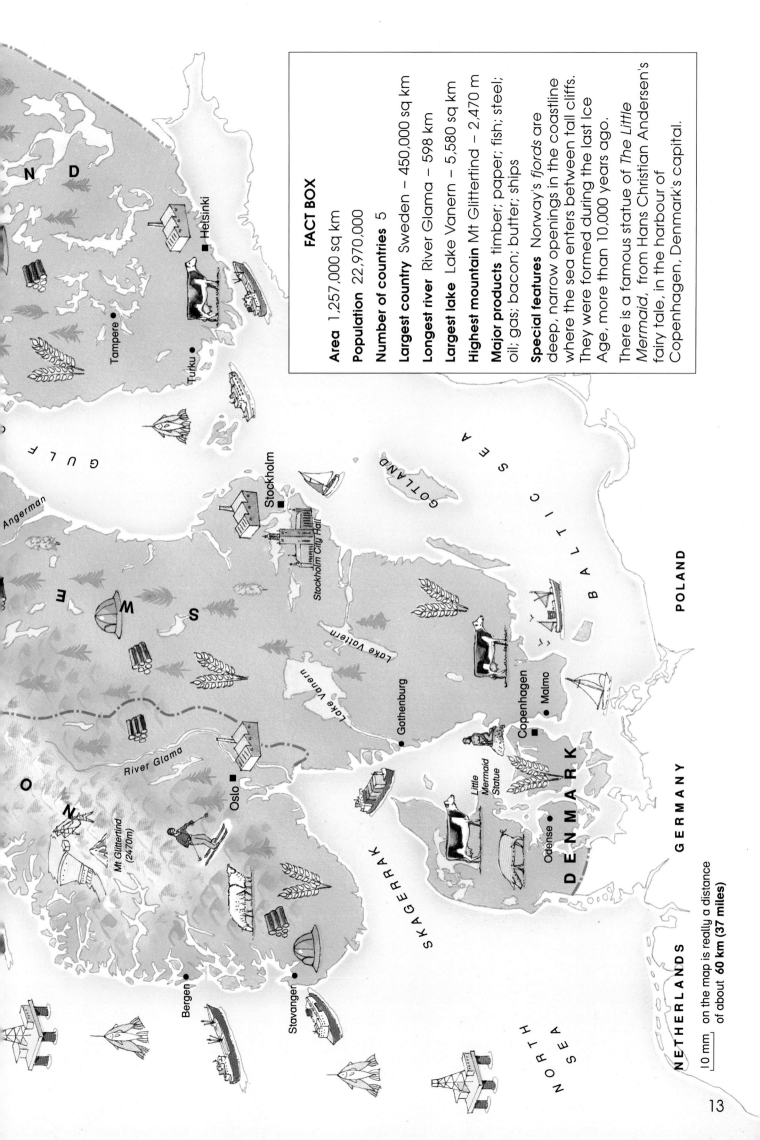

FACT BOX

Area 1,257,000 sq km

Population 22,970,000

Number of countries 5

Largest country Sweden – 450,000 sq km

Longest river River Glama – 598 km

Largest lake Lake Vanern – 5,580 sq km

Highest mountain Mt Glittertind – 2,470 m

Major products timber; paper; fish; steel; oil; gas; bacon; butter; ships

Special features Norway's *fjords* are deep, narrow openings in the coastline where the sea enters between tall cliffs. They were formed during the last Ice Age, more than 10,000 years ago.

There is a famous statue of *The Little Mermaid*, from Hans Christian Andersen's fairy tale, in the harbour of Copenhagen, Denmark's capital.

10 mm on the map is really a distance of about **60 km (37 miles)**

Central Europe

Central Europe ranges from very
low-lying land in the west, to
high mountains and forests in
the south. There is a lot of industry,
which uses the area's large
supplies of coal for fuel.

DENMARK

SWEDEN

NORTH SEA

Kiel •

• Hamburg

NETHERLANDS
Lake IJssel

Amsterdam ■

• Hanover

Berlin ■

Rotterdam •

Antwerp •

River Ruhr

Brussels ■

• Dusseldorf

G E R M A N Y

• Cologne

B E L G I U M

• Bonn

Prague •

CZECH
REPUBL

River Elbe

River Mosel

Luxembourg ■

River Rhine

• Frankfurt

River Main

River Vltava

LUXEMBOURG

F R A N C E

River Danube

BLACK FOREST

Great Abbey
of Melk

Vie

• Munich

Lake Constance

Neuschwanstein Castle

• Salzburg

• Zurich

• Innsbruck

■ Berne

A L P S

A U S T R I A

SWITZERLAND

LIECHTENSTEIN

Lake Geneva

Geneva •

*Gross Glockner
(3797m)*

*Matterhorn
(4478m)*

Wolfgang Amadeus *Mozart* was
born in Salzburg, Austria,
in 1756. He composed his
first piece of music when he
was only five years old.

ADRIATIC SEA

I T A L Y

10 mm on the map is really a distance
of about **50 km (31 miles)**

14

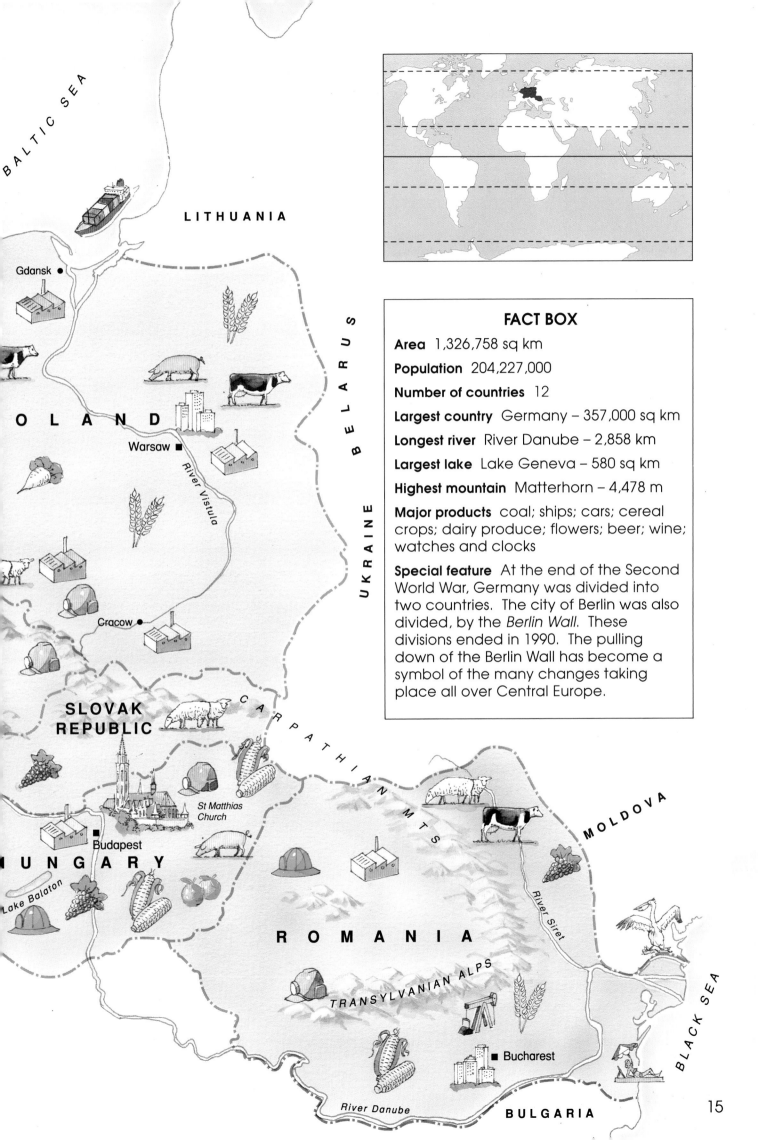

BALTIC SEA

LITHUANIA

Gdansk •

O L A N D

Warsaw ■

River Vistula

Cracow •

BELARUS

UKRAINE

FACT BOX

Area 1,326,758 sq km

Population 204,227,000

Number of countries 12

Largest country Germany – 357,000 sq km

Longest river River Danube – 2,858 km

Largest lake Lake Geneva – 580 sq km

Highest mountain Matterhorn – 4,478 m

Major products coal; ships; cars; cereal crops; dairy produce; flowers; beer; wine; watches and clocks

Special feature At the end of the Second World War, Germany was divided into two countries. The city of Berlin was also divided, by the *Berlin Wall*. These divisions ended in 1990. The pulling down of the Berlin Wall has become a symbol of the many changes taking place all over Central Europe.

SLOVAK REPUBLIC

CARPATHIAN MTS

St Matthias Church

MOLDOVA

Budapest ■

UNGARY

Lake Balaton

River Siret

R O M A N I A

TRANSYLVANIAN ALPS

■ Bucharest

BLACK SEA

River Danube

BULGARIA

Southern Europe

Southern Europe includes many of the countries around the Mediterranean Sea. In summer, they have sunny, warm weather. They also have long beaches and many ancient buildings to visit.

These make them very popular with holidaymakers. Many people work in the tourist trade. Others work in offices or factories, or as farmers.

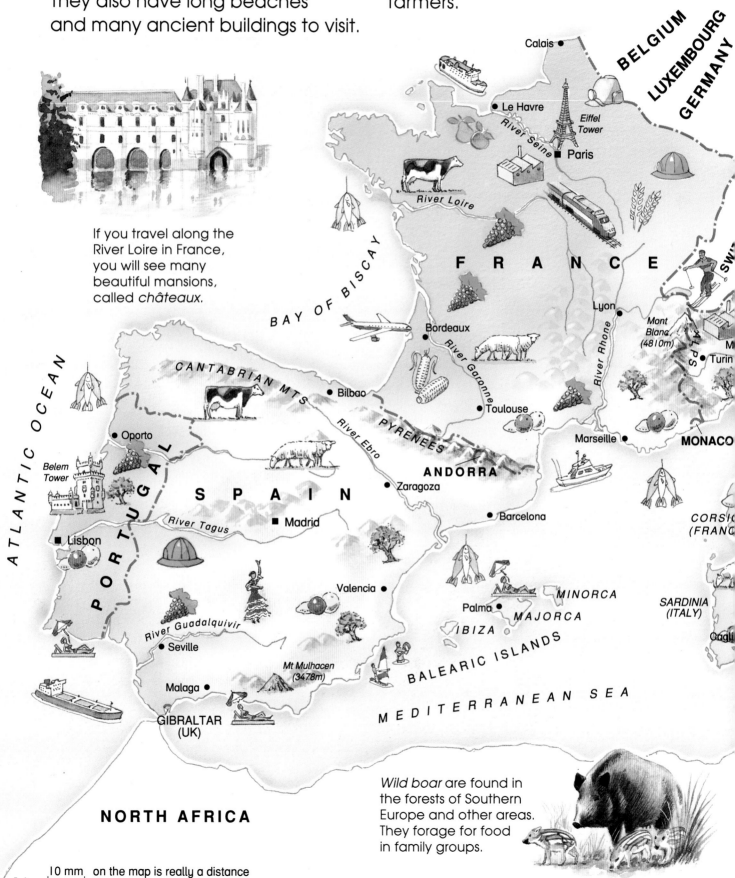

If you travel along the River Loire in France, you will see many beautiful mansions, called *châteaux*.

Calais

BELGIUM
LUXEMBOURG
GERMANY

Le Havre

Eiffel Tower

River Seine

Paris

River Loire

F R A N C E

SW

BAY OF BISCAY

Bordeaux

Lyon

Mont Blanc (4810m)

ALPS

River Garonne

River Rhone

Toulouse

M

Turin

ATLANTIC OCEAN

CANTABRIAN MTS

Bilbao

PYRENEES

River Ebro

ANDORRA

Marseille

MONACO

Oporto

Belem Tower

P O R T U G A L

S P A I N

Zaragoza

Barcelona

CORSIC
(FRANC

River Tagus

Madrid

Lisbon

Valencia

MINORCA

Palma

MAJORCA

SARDINIA
(ITALY)

IBIZA

River Guadalquivir

Seville

BALEARIC ISLANDS

Cagli

Mt Mulhacen
(3478m)

Malaga

M E D I T E R R A N E A N   S E A

GIBRALTAR
(UK)

NORTH AFRICA

Wild boar are found in the forests of Southern Europe and other areas. They forage for food in family groups.

⊢10 mm⊣ on the map is really a distance of about **82 km (51 miles)**

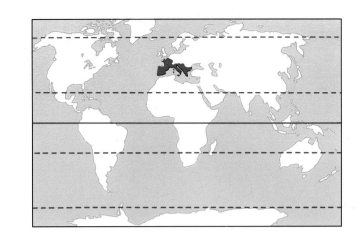

FACT BOX

Area 1,973,516 sq km

Population 208,915,000

Largest country France – 547,000 sq km

Longest river River Tagus – 1,006 km

Largest lake Lake Garda – 370 sq km

Highest mountain Mont Blanc – 4,810 m

Major products cereal crops; wine; cheese; citrus fruit; cars; olives; olive oil; fish; cork; tomatoes

Special feature The French train, the *TGV*, is the fastest passenger train in the world. It races along at up to 300 kph. The initials TGV stand for *Train à Grande Vitesse.* This is French for 'high-speed train'.

The *Vatican City* in Rome is the world's smallest country. It is the headquarters of the Roman Catholic Church. *St Peter's Basilica* inside the Vatican is the world's biggest church.

AUSTRIA   HUNGARY

DOLOMITES
Como
Lake Garda
Venice
River Po

■ Zagreb
River Sava
River Danube

ROMANIA

BLACK SEA

SAN MARINO
Florence
River Arno
River Tiber

(YUGOSLAVIA)
Sarajevo ■
Belgrade ■

BULGARIA
BALKAN MTS
■ Sofia
Mt Musala
(2925m)

ITALY
APENNINES
Colosseum
Rome ■
VATICAN CITY

ADRIATIC SEA

4   4

5

Tirana ■
ALBANIA

• Thessaloniki

TURKEY

Naples ●
Mt Vesuvius
(1277m)

GREECE
PINDUS MTS

Mt Olympus
(2917m)

AEGEAN SEA

CORFU

Parthenon

● Palermo
Mt Etna
(3340m)

IONIAN SEA

Athens ■

SICILY

MALTA

RHODES

1 REPUBLIC OF SLOVENIA
2 REPUBLIC OF CROATIA
3 REPUBLIC OF BOSNIA AND HERZEGOVINA
4 FEDERAL REPUBLIC OF YUGOSLAVIA
5 REPUBLIC OF MACEDONIA

CRETE

Eastern Europe & Northern Asia

This huge area is divided into Europe and Asia by the Ural Mountains. Most people live in the west. They work on farms and in factories. Large forests stretch across the north. Winters here are very cold. Many different people live in Eastern Europe and Northern Asia. They speak over 100 languages between them.

1 ESTONIA
2 LATVIA
3 LITHUANIA
4 MOLDOVA
5 GEORGIA
6 ARMENIA
7 AZERBAIJAN
8 TADJIKISTAN

Dancers from the *Kirov* and *Bolshoi ballet companies* perform all over the world. They are famous for their elegant dancing.

10 mm on the map is really a distance of about **220 km (136 miles)**

18

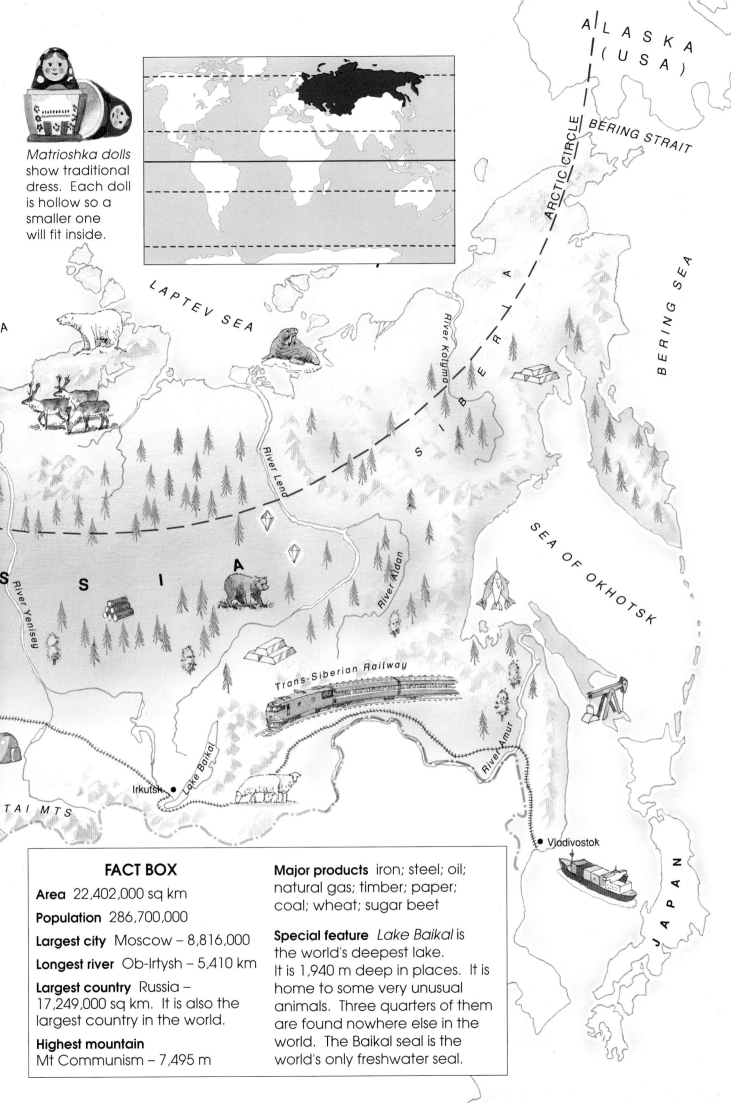

Matrioshka dolls show traditional dress. Each doll is hollow so a smaller one will fit inside.

ALASKA (USA)

BERING STRAIT

ARCTIC CIRCLE

BERING SEA

LAPTEV SEA

SIBERIA

River Kolyma

River Lena

River Aldan

RUSSIA

River Yenisey

SEA OF OKHOTSK

Trans-Siberian Railway

River Amur

Lake Baikal

Irkutsk

TAI MTS

Vladivostok

JAPAN

FACT BOX

Area 22,402,000 sq km

Population 286,700,000

Largest city Moscow – 8,816,000

Longest river Ob-Irtysh – 5,410 km

Largest country Russia – 17,249,000 sq km. It is also the largest country in the world.

Highest mountain Mt Communism – 7,495 m

Major products iron; steel; oil; natural gas; timber; paper; coal; wheat; sugar beet

Special feature *Lake Baikal* is the world's deepest lake. It is 1,940 m deep in places. It is home to some very unusual animals. Three quarters of them are found nowhere else in the world. The Baikal seal is the world's only freshwater seal.

Canada

Canada is the largest country on the continent of North America. The land ranges from wheat fields and plains in the south to Arctic ice and snow in the far north, and great mountains in the west.

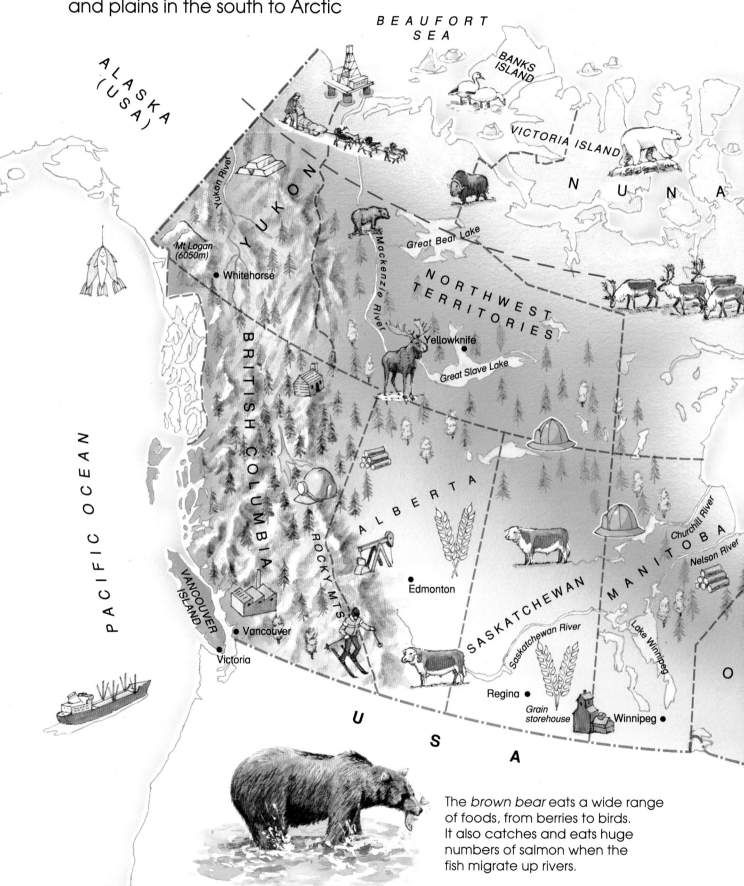

BEAUFORT SEA

BANKS ISLAND

VICTORIA ISLAND

NUNA

A L A S K A (U S A)

Yukon River

Mt Logan (6050m)

● Whitehorse

Y U K O N

Mackenzie River

Great Bear Lake

N O R T H W E S T T E R R I T O R I E S

Yellowknife

Great Slave Lake

B R I T I S H   C O L U M B I A

P A C I F I C   O C E A N

VANCOUVER ISLAND

● Vancouver

Victoria

R O C K Y   M T S

A L B E R T A

● Edmonton

S A S K A T C H E W A N

Saskatchewan River

M A N I T O B A

Churchill River

Nelson River

Lake Winnipeg

O

Regina ●

Grain storehouse

Winnipeg ●

U   S   A

The *brown bear* eats a wide range of foods, from berries to birds. It also catches and eats huge numbers of salmon when the fish migrate up rivers.

10 mm on the map is really a distance of about **150 km (93 miles)**

20

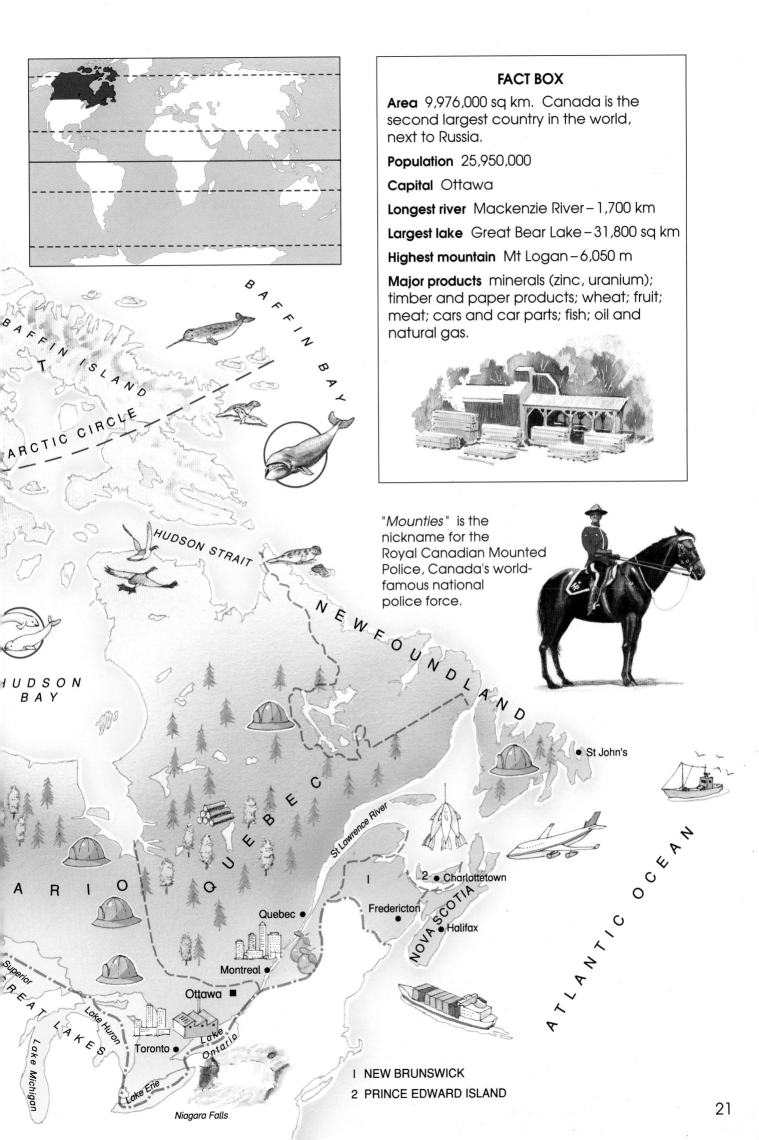

FACT BOX

Area 9,976,000 sq km. Canada is the second largest country in the world, next to Russia.

Population 25,950,000

Capital Ottawa

Longest river Mackenzie River – 1,700 km

Largest lake Great Bear Lake – 31,800 sq km

Highest mountain Mt Logan – 6,050 m

Major products minerals (zinc, uranium); timber and paper products; wheat; fruit; meat; cars and car parts; fish; oil and natural gas.

"Mounties" is the nickname for the Royal Canadian Mounted Police, Canada's world-famous national police force.

BAFFIN ISLAND

BAFFIN BAY

ARCTIC CIRCLE

HUDSON STRAIT

HUDSON BAY

NEWFOUNDLAND

QUEBEC

ARIO

St Lawrence River

• St John's

2 • Charlottetown

Fredericton

NOVA SCOTIA

Quebec •

Montreal •

Ottawa ■

Halifax

ATLANTIC OCEAN

Superior

GREAT LAKES

Lake Huron

Lake Michigan

Lake Ontario

Toronto •

Lake Erie

Niagara Falls

1 NEW BRUNSWICK
2 PRINCE EDWARD ISLAND

21

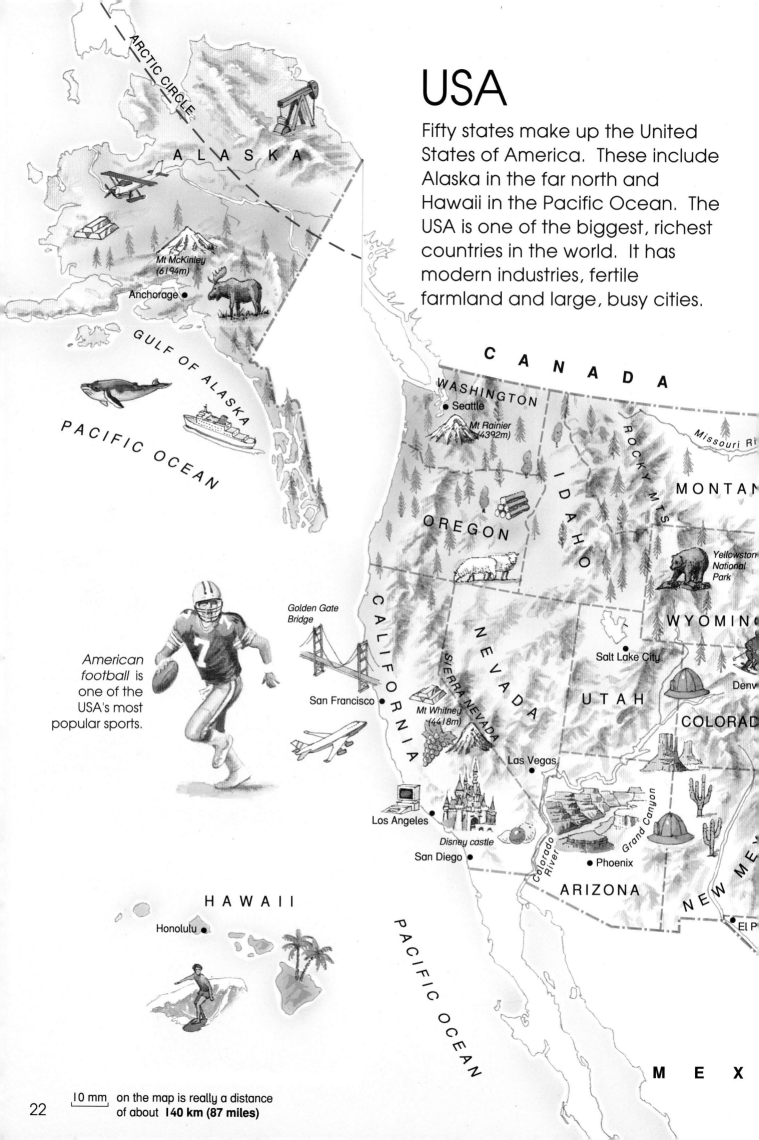

USA

Fifty states make up the United States of America. These include Alaska in the far north and Hawaii in the Pacific Ocean. The USA is one of the biggest, richest countries in the world. It has modern industries, fertile farmland and large, busy cities.

ARCTIC CIRCLE

A L A S K A

Mt McKinley
(6194m)

Anchorage ●

GULF OF ALASKA

PACIFIC OCEAN

C A N A D A

WASHINGTON
● Seattle
Mt Rainier
(4392m)

Missouri Ri

R
O
C
K
Y

M
T
S

MONTAN

O R E G O N

I D A H O

Yellowston
National
Park

WYOMING

American football is one of the USA's most popular sports.

Golden Gate Bridge

San Francisco ●

C
A
L
I
F
O
R
N
I
A

N
E
V
A
D
A

S
I
E
R
R
A
N
E
V
A
D
A

Mt Whitney
(4418m)

Salt Lake City ●

U T A H

COLORAD

Denv

Las Vegas
●

Los Angeles ●

Disney castle

San Diego ●

Colorado River

Grand Canyon

Phoenix ●

A R I Z O N A

N
E
W

M
E

El P

H A W A I I

Honolulu ●

P
A
C
I
F
I
C

O
C
E
A
N

M E X

|10 mm| on the map is really a distance of about **140 km (87 miles)**

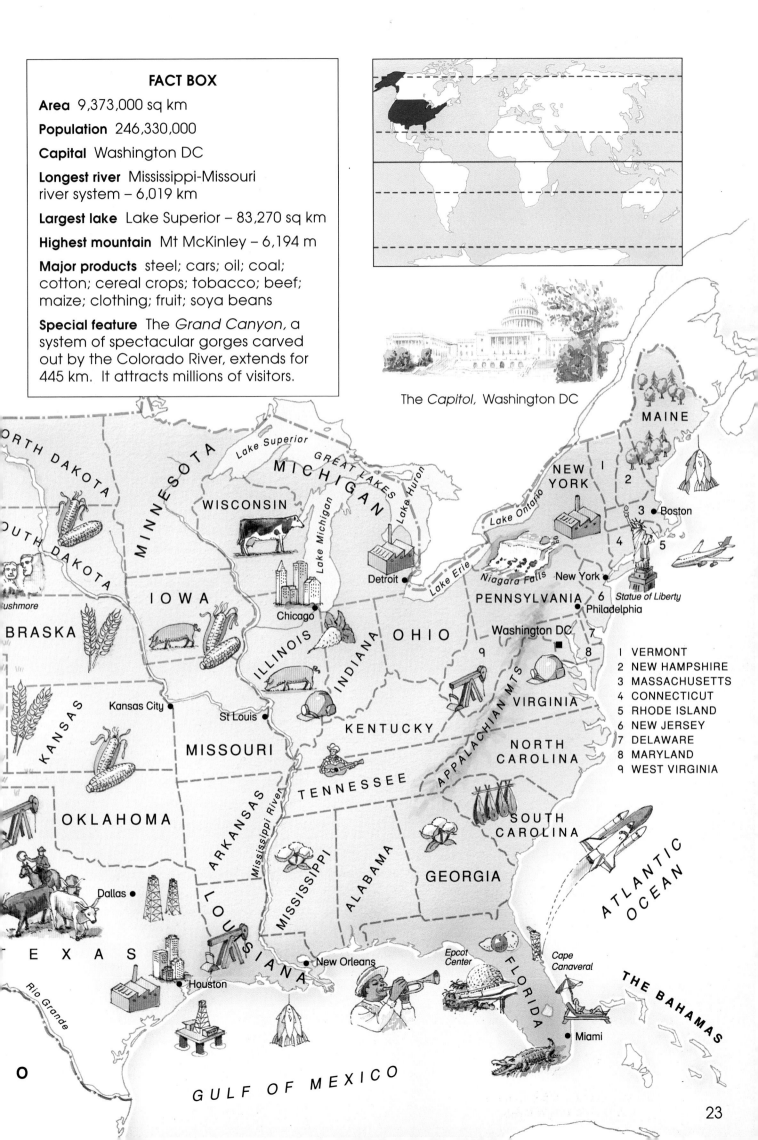

FACT BOX

Area 9,373,000 sq km

Population 246,330,000

Capital Washington DC

Longest river Mississippi-Missouri river system – 6,019 km

Largest lake Lake Superior – 83,270 sq km

Highest mountain Mt McKinley – 6,194 m

Major products steel; cars; oil; coal; cotton; cereal crops; tobacco; beef; maize; clothing; fruit; soya beans

Special feature The *Grand Canyon,* a system of spectacular gorges carved out by the Colorado River, extends for 445 km. It attracts millions of visitors.

The *Capitol,* Washington DC

MAINE

Lake Superior

GREAT LAKES

MICHIGAN

NORTH DAKOTA

SOUTH DAKOTA

Rushmore

MINNESOTA

WISCONSIN

Lake Michigan

Lake Huron

NEW YORK

Lake Ontario

Niagara Falls

Lake Erie

Detroit

IOWA

Chicago

BRASKA

ILLINOIS

INDIANA

OHIO

PENNSYLVANIA

Washington DC

New York

Statue of Liberty

Philadelphia

1

2

3 • Boston

4

5

6

7

8

9

Kansas City

St Louis

KANSAS

MISSOURI

KENTUCKY

VIRGINIA

NORTH CAROLINA

1 VERMONT
2 NEW HAMPSHIRE
3 MASSACHUSETTS
4 CONNECTICUT
5 RHODE ISLAND
6 NEW JERSEY
7 DELAWARE
8 MARYLAND
9 WEST VIRGINIA

APPALACHIAN MTS

OKLAHOMA

ARKANSAS

Mississippi River

TENNESSEE

SOUTH CAROLINA

Dallas •

MISSISSIPPI

ALABAMA

GEORGIA

ATLANTIC OCEAN

TEXAS

Rio Grande

LOUISIANA

New Orleans

Houston

Epcot Center

FLORIDA

Cape Canaveral

THE BAHAMAS

O

Miami

GULF OF MEXICO

23

Caribbean & Latin America

Latin America is made up of Mexico, the continent of South America, and Central America – the thin strip of countries joining South America to North America.

The region has a varied landscape, ranging from deserts to jungles and from high mountains to plains. The Caribbean islands to the east, sometimes called the West Indies, are popular with tourists, who come to enjoy the mild winter weather.

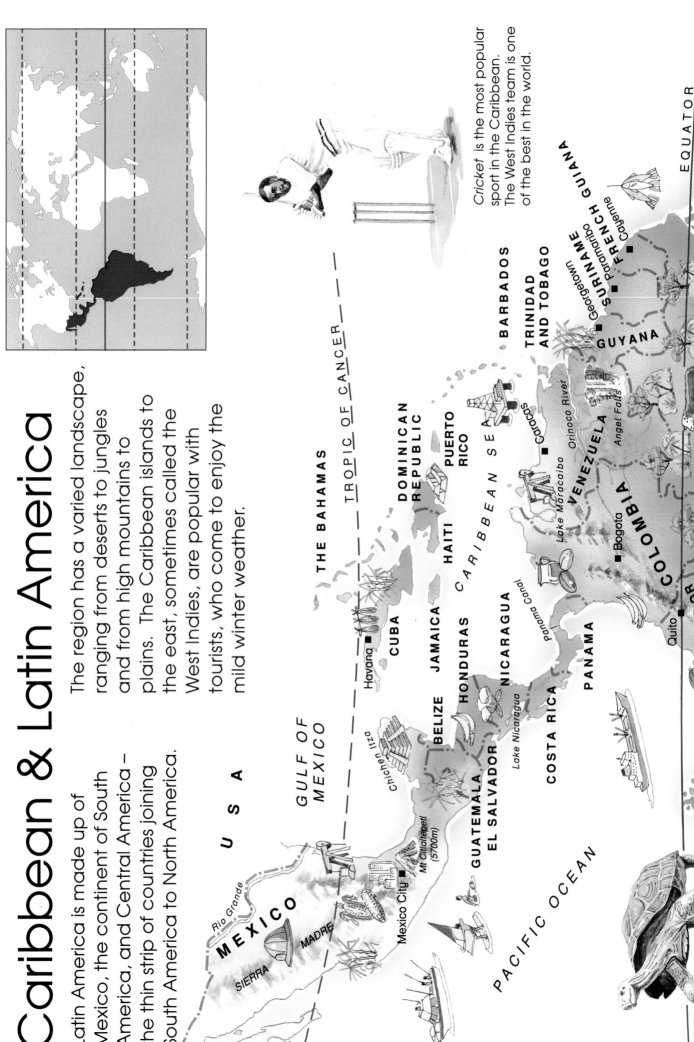

Cricket is the most popular sport in the Caribbean. The West Indies team is one of the best in the world.

EQUATOR

TROPIC OF CANCER

THE BAHAMAS

CUBA
Havana ■

DOMINICAN REPUBLIC
HAITI
JAMAICA
PUERTO RICO

CARIBBEAN SEA

BARBADOS

TRINIDAD AND TOBAGO

GUYANA
Georgetown ■
SURINAME
Paramaribo ■
FRENCH GUIANA
Cayenne ■

Caracas ■
VENEZUELA
Orinoco River
Angel Falls
Lake Maracaibo

COLOMBIA
Bogotá ■

Quito ■

GULF OF MEXICO

U S A

Rio Grande

M E X I C O
SIERRA MADRE
Mexico City ■
Mt Citlaltepetl (5700m)
Chichen Itzá

BELIZE
GUATEMALA
EL SALVADOR
HONDURAS
NICARAGUA
Lake Nicaragua
COSTA RICA
PANAMA
Panama Canal

PACIFIC OCEAN

24

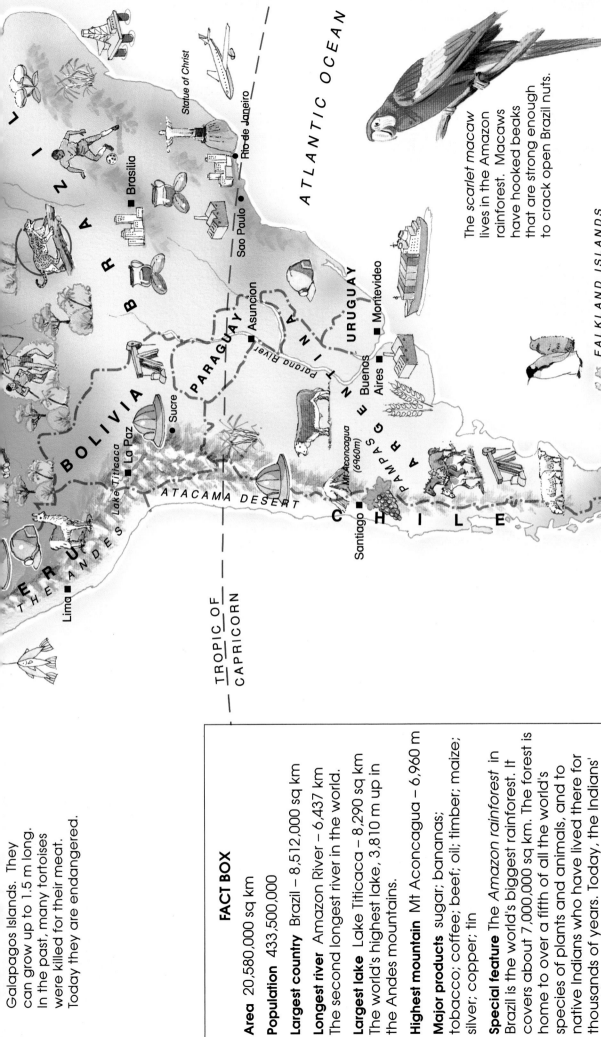

Galapagos Islands. They can grow up to 1.5 m long. In the past, many tortoises were killed for their meat. Today they are endangered.

The *scarlet macaw* lives in the Amazon rainforest. Macaws have hooked beaks that are strong enough to crack open Brazil nuts.

ATLANTIC OCEAN

Statue of Christ

Rio de Janeiro

Sao Paulo

Brasilia

B R A Z I L

Asuncion

PARAGUAY

Parana River

URUGUAY

Montevideo

A R G E N T I N A

Buenos Aires

P A M P A S

BOLIVIA

Sucre

La Paz

Lake Titicaca

THE ANDES

P E R U

Lima

ATACAMA DESERT

Mt Aconcagua (6960m)

Santiago

C H I L E

FALKLAND ISLANDS

TIERRA DEL FUEGO

CAPE HORN

TROPIC OF CAPRICORN

FACT BOX

Area 20,580,000 sq km

Population 433,500,000

Largest country Brazil – 8,512,000 sq km

Longest river Amazon River – 6,437 km
The second longest river in the world.

Largest lake Lake Titicaca – 8,290 sq km
The world's highest lake, 3,810 m up in the Andes mountains.

Highest mountain Mt Aconcagua – 6,960 m

Major products sugar; bananas; tobacco; coffee; beef; oil; timber; maize; silver; copper; tin

Special feature The *Amazon rainforest* in Brazil is the world's biggest rainforest. It covers about 7,000,000 sq km. The forest is home to over a fifth of all the world's species of plants and animals, and to native Indians who have lived there for thousands of years. Today, the Indians' way of life and the forest's amazing wildlife are under threat. A huge patch of rainforest is cut down every day to make space for mining and ranching.

10 mm on the map is really a distance of about **316 km (196 miles)**

Africa

Africa is the second largest continent. It has hot, steamy rainforests near the equator, tropical grasslands, deserts and mountains. Many different peoples live in Africa, such as Arabs in the north and Pygmy tribes in Zaire.

Together, the people of Africa make up about a tenth of the world's population. Some people work in cities such as Nairobi, but many others are nomads or farmers and are very poor.

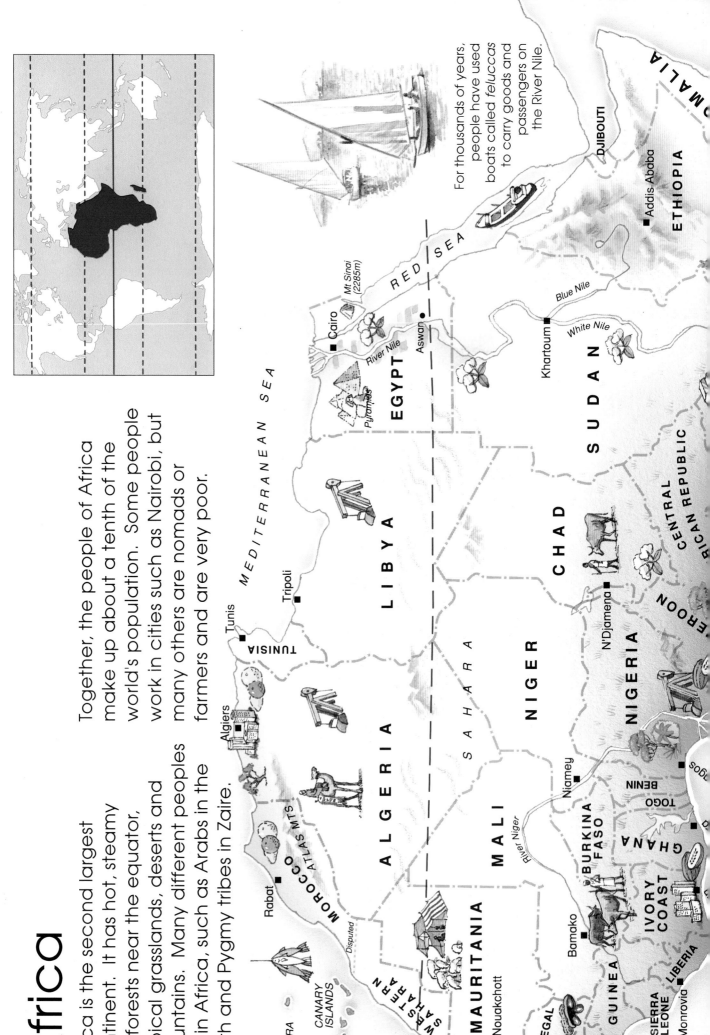

For thousands of years, people have used boats called *feluccas* to carry goods and passengers on the River Nile.

MEDITERRANEAN SEA

RED SEA

Cairo

Mt Sinai (2285m)

Aswan

River Nile

Blue Nile

White Nile

Khartoum

EGYPT

SUDAN

ETHIOPIA

Addis Ababa

DJIBOUTI

SOMALIA

Pyramids

LIBYA

Tripoli

Tunis

TUNISIA

Algiers

ALGERIA

ATLAS MTS

MOROCCO

Rabat

Disputed

WESTERN SAHARA

SAHARA

NIGER

CHAD

N'Djamena

NIGERIA

CAMEROON

CENTRAL AFRICAN REPUBLIC

Niamey

BENIN

TOGO

GHANA

BURKINA FASO

IVORY COAST

MALI

River Niger

Bamako

MAURITANIA

Nouakchott

SENEGAL

Dakar

THE GAMBIA

GUINEA BISSAU

GUINEA

SIERRA LEONE

LIBERIA

Monrovia

Lagos

MADEIRA

CANARY ISLANDS

TROPIC OF CANCER

ATLAN

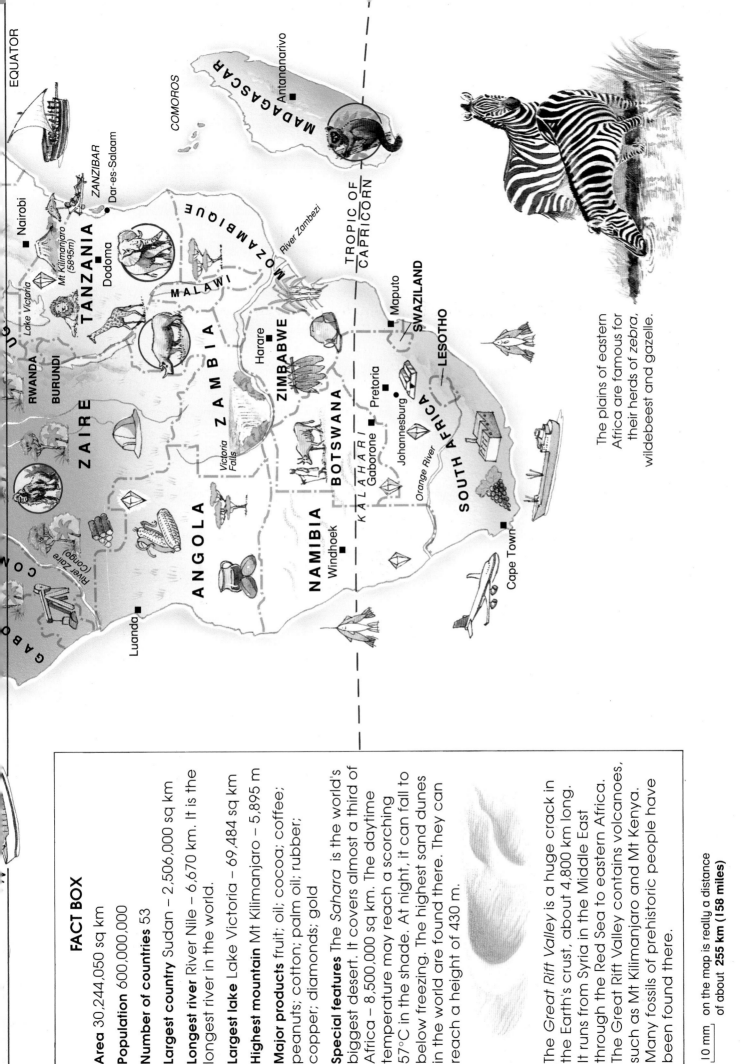

EQUATOR

COMOROS

MADAGASCAR

■ Antananarivo

Nairobi ■

ZANZIBAR

Dar-es-Salaam

Mt Kilimanjaro
(5895m)

TANZANIA

Lake Victoria

Dodoma

RWANDA

BURUNDI

ZAIRE

MOZAMBIQUE

River Zambezi

MALAWI

ZAMBIA

Harare

ZIMBABWE

Victoria
Falls

TROPIC OF
CAPRICORN

Maputo ■

SWAZILAND

LESOTHO

ANGOLA

NAMIBIA

Windhoek

BOTSWANA

Gaborone

KALAHARI

Pretoria
● Johannesburg

Orange River

SOUTH AFRICA

Cape Town ■

Luanda ■

River Zaïre
(Congo)

GABON

CON...

The plains of eastern
Africa are famous for
their herds of zebra,
wildebeest and gazelle.

FACT BOX

Area 30,244,050 sq km

Population 600,000,000

Number of countries 53

Largest country Sudan – 2,506,000 sq km

Longest river River Nile – 6,670 km. It is the
longest river in the world.

Largest lake Lake Victoria – 69,484 sq km

Highest mountain Mt Kilimanjaro – 5,895 m

Major products fruit; oil; cocoa; coffee;
peanuts; cotton; palm oil; rubber;
copper; diamonds; gold

Special features The *Sahara* is the world's
biggest desert. It covers almost a third of
Africa – 8,500,000 sq km. The daytime
temperature may reach a scorching
57°C in the shade. At night, it can fall to
below freezing. The highest sand dunes
in the world are found there. They can
reach a height of 430 m.

The *Great Rift Valley* is a huge crack in
the Earth's crust, about 4,800 km long.
It runs from Syria in the Middle East
through the Red Sea to eastern Africa.
The Great Rift Valley contains volcanoes,
such as Mt Kilimanjaro and Mt Kenya.
Many fossils of prehistoric people have
been found there.

10 mm ⊢—⊣ on the map is really a distance
of about **255 km (158 miles)**

The Middle East

Where the continents of Europe, Africa and Asia meet lies a region often called the Middle East. The countries around the Mediterranean Sea have hot, dry summers but sometimes cold winters. Further south, most of the land is desert. Huge amounts of oil have been found under the desert and out at sea.

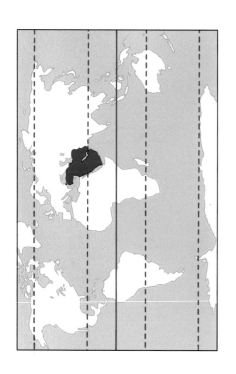

Oil is pumped from under the desert and flows along huge pipes to the coast. Here it is refined and loaded into supertankers.

AFGHANISTAN

CASPIAN SEA

IRAN

Tehran

AZERBAIJAN

ARMENIA

ELBURZ MTS

Lake Urmia

ZAG

Mt Ararat (5165m)

GEORGIA

Lake Van

River Tigris

River Euphrates

Baghdad

TURKEY

SYRIA

IRAQ

BLACK SEA

Ankara

Damascus

Amman

River Jordan

Blue Mosque

Istanbul

LEBANON

Beirut

Dead Sea

CYPRUS

Nicosia

ISRAEL

Jerusalem

GREECE

MEDITERRANEAN SEA

Port Said

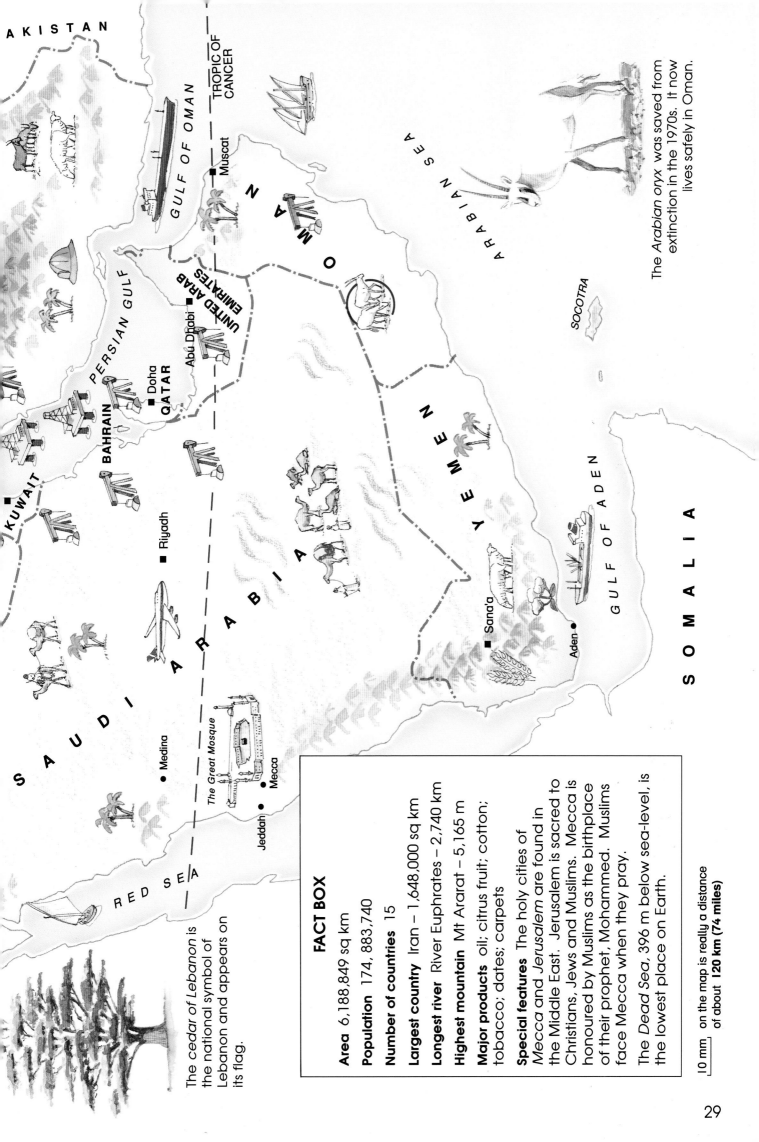

P A K I S T A N

TROPIC OF CANCER

GULF OF OMAN

Muscat ■

O M A N

PERSIAN GULF

■ Doha QATAR

Abu Dhabi ■
UNITED ARAB
EMIRATES

BAHRAIN

KUWAIT

■ Riyadh

ARABIAN SEA

SOCOTRA

The *Arabian oryx* was saved from extinction in the 1970s. It now lives safely in Oman.

S A U D I   A R A B I A

Y E M E N

GULF OF ADEN

S O M A L I A

Sana'a ■

Aden ●

● Medina

The Great Mosque

● Mecca

● Jeddah

RED SEA

The *cedar of Lebanon* is the national symbol of Lebanon and appears on its flag.

FACT BOX

Area 6,188,849 sq km

Population 174,883,740

Number of countries 15

Largest country Iran – 1,648,000 sq km

Longest river River Euphrates – 2,740 km

Highest mountain Mt Ararat – 5,165 m

Major products oil; citrus fruit; cotton; tobacco; dates; carpets

Special features The holy cities of *Mecca* and *Jerusalem* are found in the Middle East. Jerusalem is sacred to Christians, Jews and Muslims. Mecca is honoured by Muslims as the birthplace of their prophet, Mohammed. Muslims face Mecca when they pray.

The *Dead Sea*, 396 m below sea-level, is the lowest place on Earth.

|10 mm| on the map is really a distance of about **120 km (74 miles)**

Southern Asia

About one fifth of all the people in the world live in Southern Asia. Many of them are very poor. Some live in small villages in the countryside and work as farmers. Rice is the most important crop of Southern Asia. The farmers rely on the heavy monsoon rains, which fall from June to November, to make their crops grow. If there is no rain, the crops fail. If the rain is too heavy, there are terrible floods when the rivers overflow. Few people live in the north of the area, where it is very mountainous.

These dancers come from southern India. The style of dance is called *Kathakali*.

FACT BOX

Area 5,815,298 sq km

Population 1,098,493,000

Number of countries 9

Largest country India – 3,288,000 sq km

Longest river Ganges-Brahmaputra river system – 2,900 km. The River Ganges is a sacred river to Hindus.

Highest mountain Mt Everest – 8,848 m. The highest mountain in the world, it forms part of the *Himalayas*, the highest and third longest mountain range in the world.

Major products rice; tea; nuts; dried fruit; silk; cotton; jute (for rope and cloth)

Special feature The *Taj Mahal* was built by Emperor Shah Jahan as a tomb for his wife. It was started in 1631 and is made from white marble inlaid with semi-precious stones. Sadly Shah Jahan's plan to build a similar tomb for himself in black marble was not carried out.

 10 mm on the map is really a distance of about **130 km (81 miles)**

CHINA

K2
Godwin Austen)
(8611m)

Bengal tigers are very
rare. They live in
special reserves where
they are well guarded.

HIMALAYAS

NEPAL

■ Delhi

Taj Mahal

Mt Everest
(8848m)

■ Kathmandu

■ Thimphu

BHUTAN

River Brahmaputra

CHINA

INDIA

River Ganges

BANGLADESH

■ Dhaka

MYANMAR (BURMA)

River Irrawaddy

River Salween

● Mandalay

Calcutta ●

DECCAN PLATEAU

Mt Victoria
(3053m)

THAILAND

● Hyderabad

Rangoon ■

BAY OF BENGAL

● Bangalore

Madras

ANDAMAN ISLANDS

NICOBAR ISLANDS

SRI LANKA

Colombo ■

The *Shwe Dagon Pagoda* in
Rangoon is a Buddhist
temple. Its roof is
covered with pure gold.

INDIAN OCEAN

31

South East Asia

South East Asia is made up of a small piece of mainland and many thousands of islands. It is hot and wet all year round. Much of the land is hilly or covered in thick forest. Most of the people in South East Asia are farmers and are quite poor. Brunei is the richest country in South East Asia because of its oil wells.

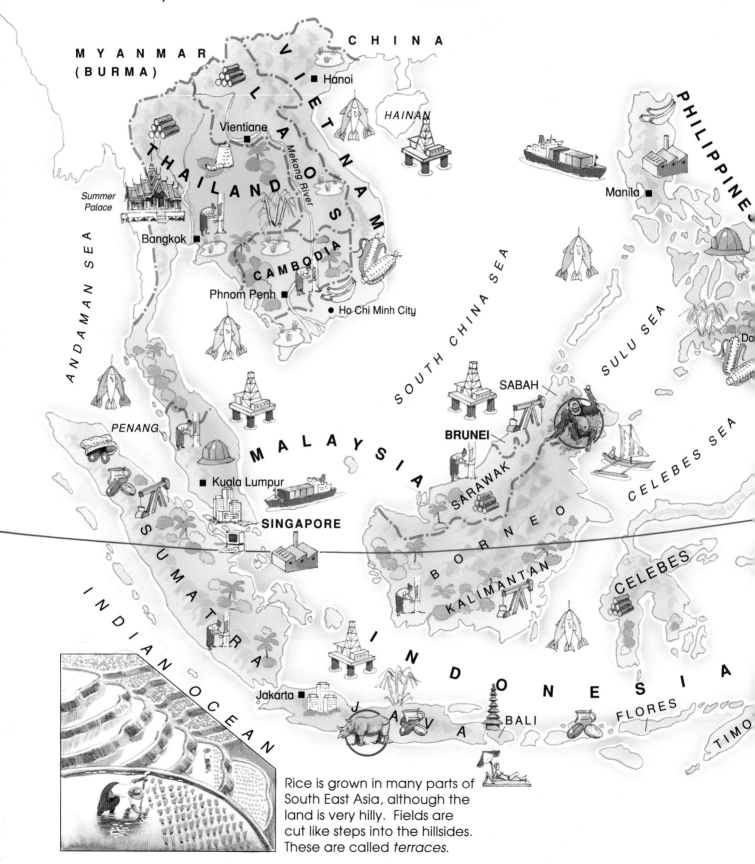

Rice is grown in many parts of South East Asia, although the land is very hilly. Fields are cut like steps into the hillsides. These are called *terraces*.

To collect *rubber*, slits are cut into the bark of a rubber tree. Sticky latex oozes out. This is made into sheets of rubber. Three quarters of the world's rubber comes from South East Asia.

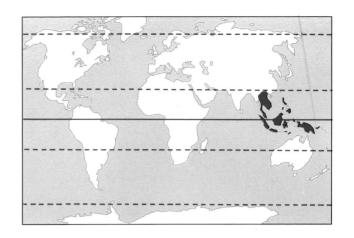

Many Chinese people live in Singapore. The *dragon dance* takes place at their popular festivals.

FACT BOX

Area 4,265,365 sq km

Population 387,553,000

Number of countries 10

Largest country Indonesia – 1,905,000 sq km

Longest river Mekong River – 4,184 km

Highest mountain Mt Puncak Jaya – 5,030 m

Major products rubber; silk; rice; oil; coffee; timber; tin; bananas

Special feature There are over 20,000 *islands* in South East Asia. The country of Indonesia alone has over 3,000. Some of the islands have cities and a large population, but most are only a few metres across. Many are really the tops of volcanoes poking out of the sea.

EQUATOR

PACIFIC OCEAN

MOLUCCAS

IRIAN JAYA

Mt Puncak Jaya (5030m)

MAOKE MTS

PAPUA NEW GUINEA

NEW IRELAND

NEW BRITAIN

BOUGAINVILLE

Port Moresby ■

ARAFURA SEA

CORAL SEA

AUSTRALIA

10 mm on the map is really a distance of about **180 km (112 miles)**

China and Korea

Over a billion people live in China, more than in any other country. Most people live in the south and east of the country. Here the land is fertile for farming. People also work in factories in the big, crowded cities. In the west, the land is very mountainous. In the north and north west, there are huge deserts.

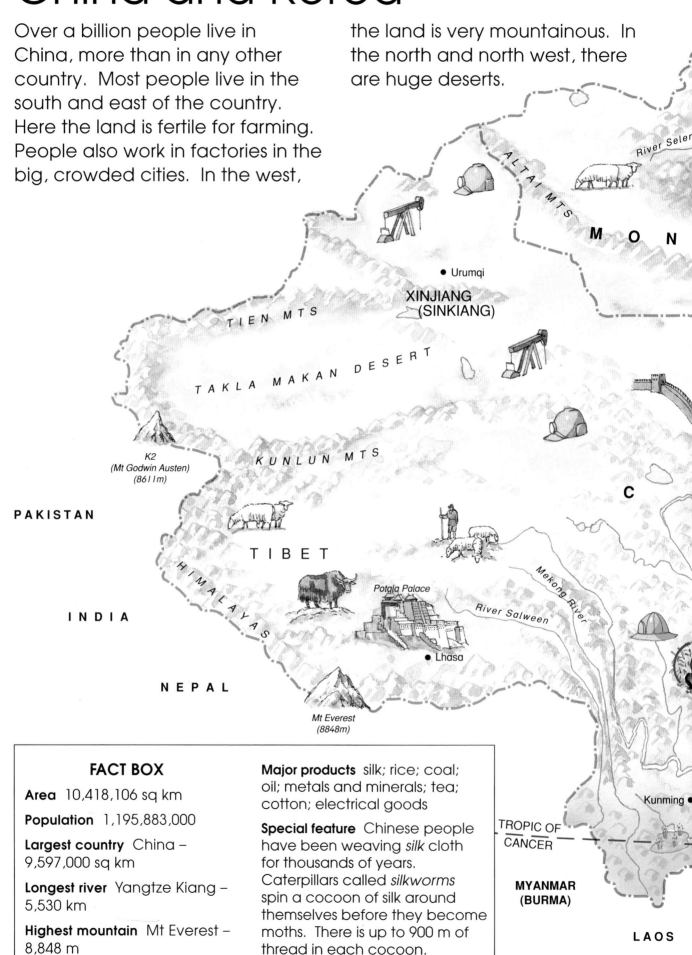

River Selen

ALTAI MTS

M O N

• Urumqi

XINJIANG
(SINKIANG)

T I E N   M T S

T A K L A   M A K A N   D E S E R T

K U N L U N   M T S

K2
(Mt Godwin Austen)
(8611m)

C

PAKISTAN

H I M A L A Y A S

T I B E T

INDIA

Potala Palace

Mekong River

River Salween

• Lhasa

NEPAL

Mt Everest
(8848m)

Kunming •

TROPIC OF
CANCER

MYANMAR
(BURMA)

LAOS

FACT BOX

Area 10,418,106 sq km

Population 1,195,883,000

Largest country China – 9,597,000 sq km

Longest river Yangtze Kiang – 5,530 km

Highest mountain Mt Everest – 8,848 m

Major products silk; rice; coal; oil; metals and minerals; tea; cotton; electrical goods

Special feature Chinese people have been weaving *silk* cloth for thousands of years. Caterpillars called *silkworms* spin a cocoon of silk around themselves before they become moths. There is up to 900 m of thread in each cocoon.

---

10 mm on the map is really a distance of about **155 km (96 miles)**

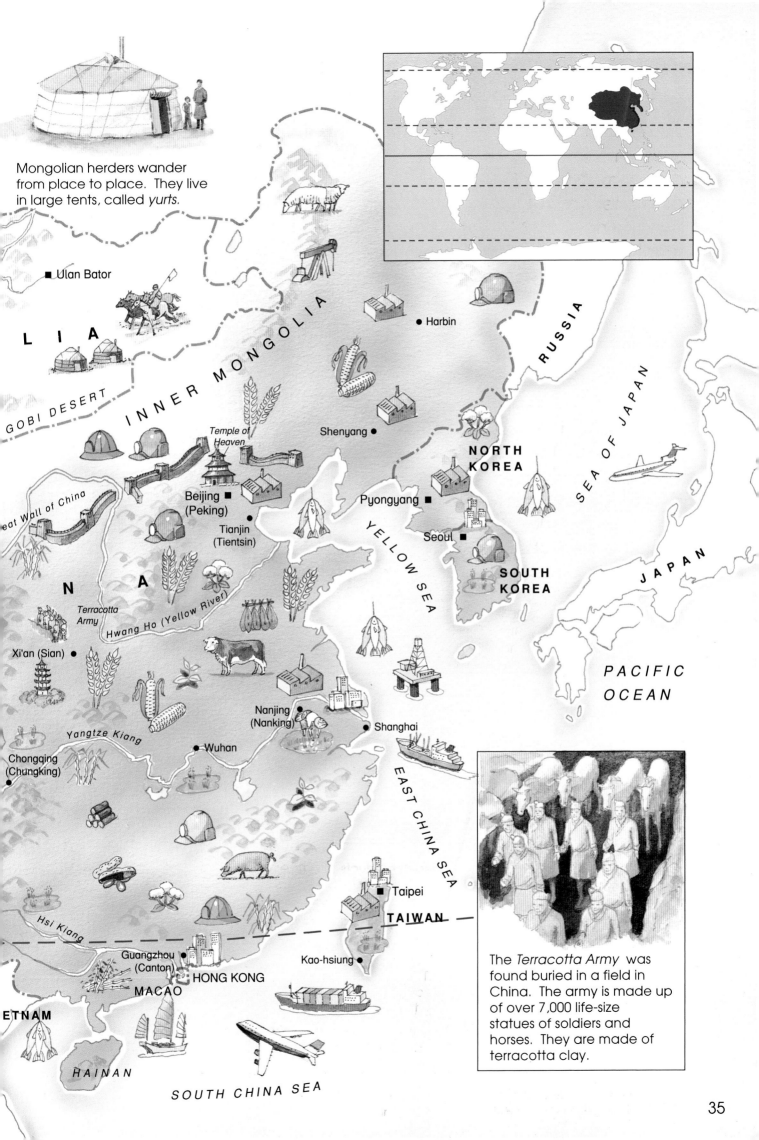

Mongolian herders wander from place to place. They live in large tents, called *yurts*.

■ Ulan Bator

L I A

GOBI DESERT

I N N E R   M O N G O L I A

• Harbin

RUSSIA

Temple of Heaven

Shenyang •

NORTH KOREA

SEA OF JAPAN

Great Wall of China

Beijing (Peking) ■

Pyongyang ■

Tianjin (Tientsin)

YELLOW SEA

Seoul ■

JAPAN

N   **A**

SOUTH KOREA

Terracotta Army

Hwang Ho (Yellow River)

Xi'an (Sian) •

PACIFIC OCEAN

Yangtze Kiang

Nanjing (Nanking) •

• Shanghai

• Wuhan

Chongqing (Chungking)

EAST CHINA SEA

Hsi Kiang

Taipei ■

TAIWAN

Guangzhou (Canton)

Kao-hsiung •

HONG KONG

MACAO

ETNAM

HAINAN

SOUTH CHINA SEA

The *Terracotta Army* was found buried in a field in China. The army is made up of over 7,000 life-size statues of soldiers and horses. They are made of terracotta clay.

Japan

Japan is an island country off the eastern coast of Asia. It is made up of four main islands and thousands of smaller ones. Much of Japan is mountainous, and there are as many as 1,500 minor earthquakes every year. Many Japanese people live in crowded cities and towns. Others work as farmers, growing rice and cereals.

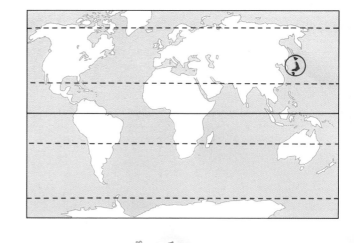

FACT BOX

Area 377,500 sq km

Population 122,610,000

Capital Tokyo

Longest river River Shinano – 367 km

Largest lake Lake Biwa – 673 sq km

Highest mountain Mt Fuji – 3,776 m

Major products ships; cars; cameras; electrical goods

Special feature *High technology:* Japan is a major industrial power. Its factories produce many electrical and electronic goods, ranging from computers to robots.

The *kimono* is the traditional dress of Japan. Today it is worn only on special occasions.

The *Bullet train* speeds along at up to 270 kph. It is one of the fastest trains in the world.

SOUTH KOREA

SEA OF JAPAN

HOKKAIDO

Sapporo ●

River Ishikari

● Hakodate

H O N S H U

River Shinano

River Tone

Golden Pavilion

Lake Biwa

Kyoto ●

Nagoya ●

Kobe ● ● Osaka

Hiroshima ●

■ Tokyo

● Yokohama

Mt Fuji (3776m)

S H I K O K U

K Y U S H U

Nagasaki ●

PACIFIC OCEAN

E A S T C H I N A S E A

|10 mm| on the map is really a distance of about **85 km (53 miles)**

New Zealand

New Zealand is in the Pacific Ocean, about 1,600 km south east of Australia. It is made up of two large islands and several smaller ones. North Island has volcanoes and hot springs. South Island has mountains, fjords and glaciers.

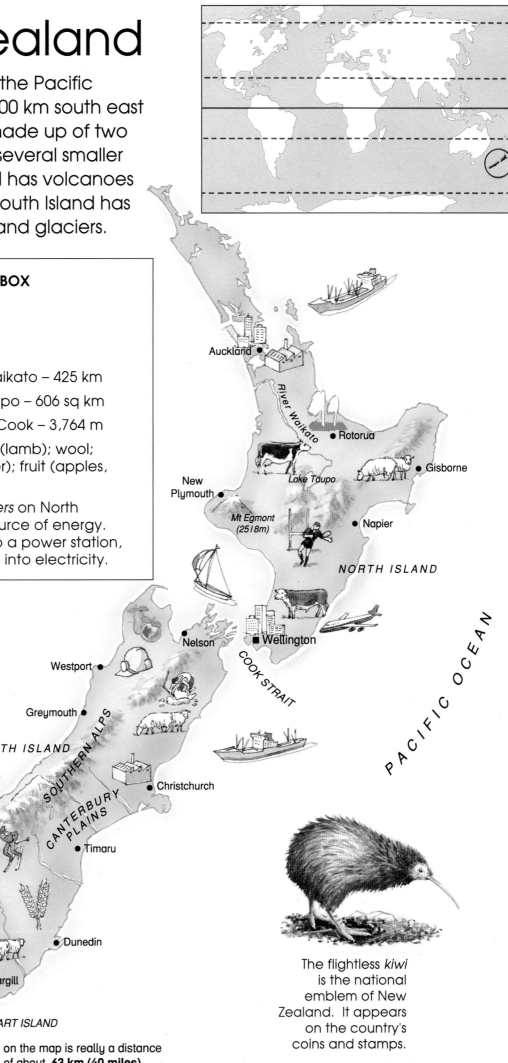

FACT BOX

Area 269,000 sq km

Population 3,290,000

Capital Wellington

Longest river River Waikato – 425 km

Largest lake Lake Taupo – 606 sq km

Highest mountain Mt Cook – 3,764 m

Major products meat (lamb); wool; dairy produce (butter); fruit (apples, kiwi fruit)

Special feature *Geysers* on North Island are a good source of energy. The steam is piped to a power station, where it is converted into electricity.

Auckland

River Waikato

Rotorua

New Plymouth

Lake Taupo

Gisborne

Mt Egmont (2518m)

Napier

NORTH ISLAND

Nelson

Wellington

COOK STRAIT

Westport

Greymouth

SOUTH ISLAND

SOUTHERN ALPS

Mt Cook (3764m)

CANTERBURY PLAINS

Christchurch

Timaru

Dunedin

Invercargill

STEWART ISLAND

TASMAN SEA

PACIFIC OCEAN

The flightless *kiwi* is the national emblem of New Zealand. It appears on the country's coins and stamps.

10 mm on the map is really a distance of about **63 km (40 miles)**

Australia

Two thirds of Australia is hot, dusty desert. Most Australians live along the coast, where the climate is more pleasant. Aborigines were the first people to live in Australia, almost 50,000 years ago. Today there are still many Aborigines, but most of the people are descended from European settlers.

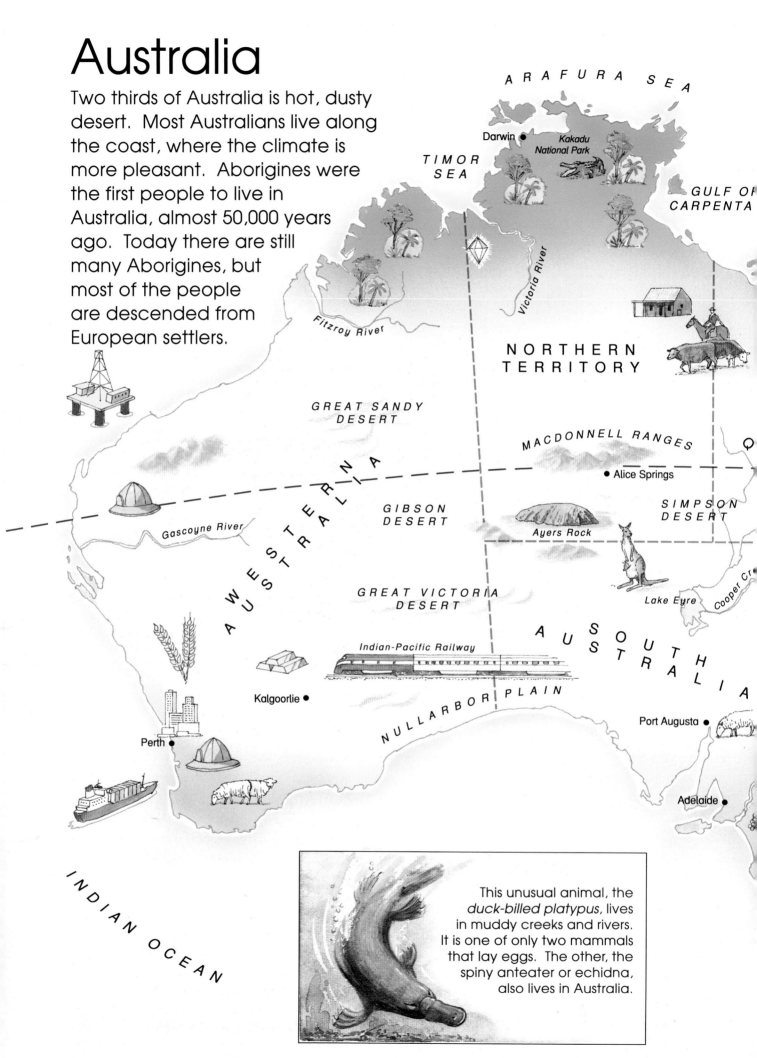

A R A F U R A   S E A

TIMOR SEA

Darwin

Kakadu National Park

GULF OF CARPENTA

Victoria River

Fitzroy River

NORTHERN TERRITORY

GREAT SANDY DESERT

MACDONNELL RANGES

Q

Alice Springs

GIBSON DESERT

SIMPSON DESERT

Gascoyne River

WESTERN AUSTRALIA

Ayers Rock

GREAT VICTORIA DESERT

Lake Eyre

Cooper Cr

SOUTH AUSTRALIA

Indian-Pacific Railway

Kalgoorlie

NULLARBOR PLAIN

Port Augusta

Perth

Adelaide

INDIAN OCEAN

This unusual animal, the *duck-billed platypus*, lives in muddy creeks and rivers. It is one of only two mammals that lay eggs. The other, the spiny anteater or echidna, also lives in Australia.

10 mm on the map is really a distance of about **138 km (86 miles)**

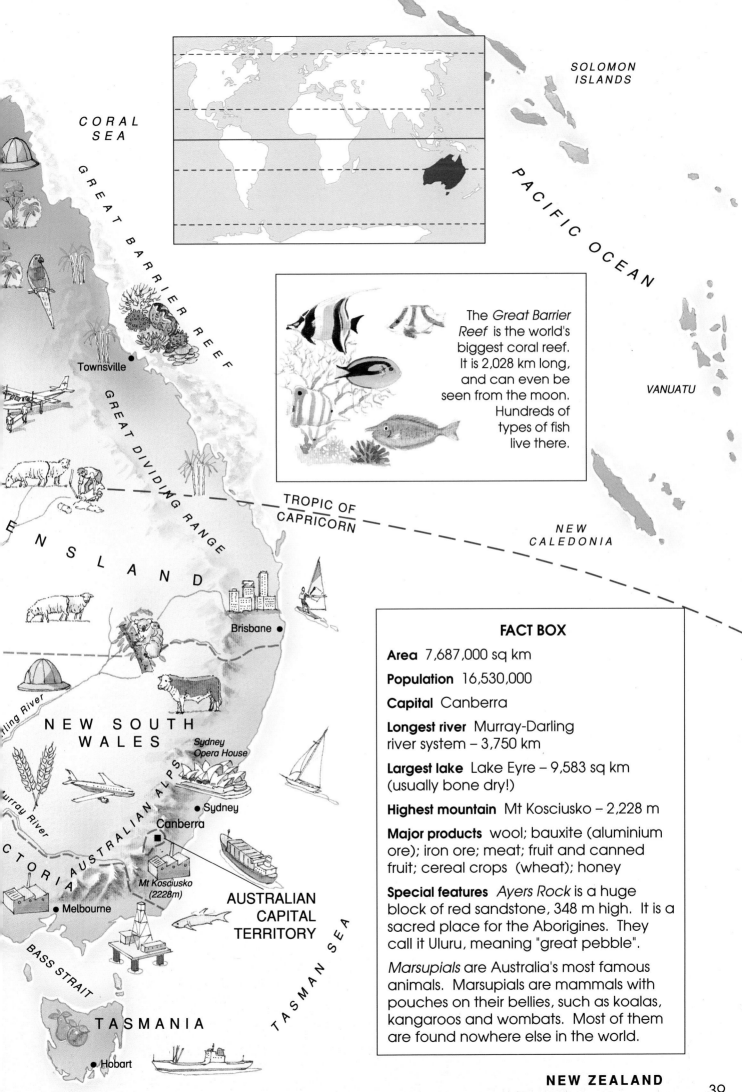

CORAL
SEA

GREAT BARRIER REEF

GREAT DIVIDING RANGE

SOLOMON
ISLANDS

PACIFIC OCEAN

VANUATU

Townsville

The *Great Barrier Reef* is the world's biggest coral reef. It is 2,028 km long, and can even be seen from the moon. Hundreds of types of fish live there.

TROPIC OF
CAPRICORN

NEW
CALEDONIA

QUEENSLAND

Brisbane

NEW SOUTH
WALES

Sydney
Opera House

AUSTRALIAN ALPS

Darling River

Murray River

Sydney

Canberra

VICTORIA

Mt Kosciusko
(2228m)

Melbourne

AUSTRALIAN
CAPITAL
TERRITORY

TASMAN SEA

BASS STRAIT

TASMANIA

Hobart

FACT BOX

Area 7,687,000 sq km

Population 16,530,000

Capital Canberra

Longest river Murray-Darling river system – 3,750 km

Largest lake Lake Eyre – 9,583 sq km (usually bone dry!)

Highest mountain Mt Kosciusko – 2,228 m

Major products wool; bauxite (aluminium ore); iron ore; meat; fruit and canned fruit; cereal crops (wheat); honey

Special features *Ayers Rock* is a huge block of red sandstone, 348 m high. It is a sacred place for the Aborigines. They call it Uluru, meaning "great pebble".

Marsupials are Australia's most famous animals. Marsupials are mammals with pouches on their bellies, such as koalas, kangaroos and wombats. Most of them are found nowhere else in the world.

NEW ZEALAND

The Poles

At the far north and the far south of the Earth, there are two huge areas of ice and snow.

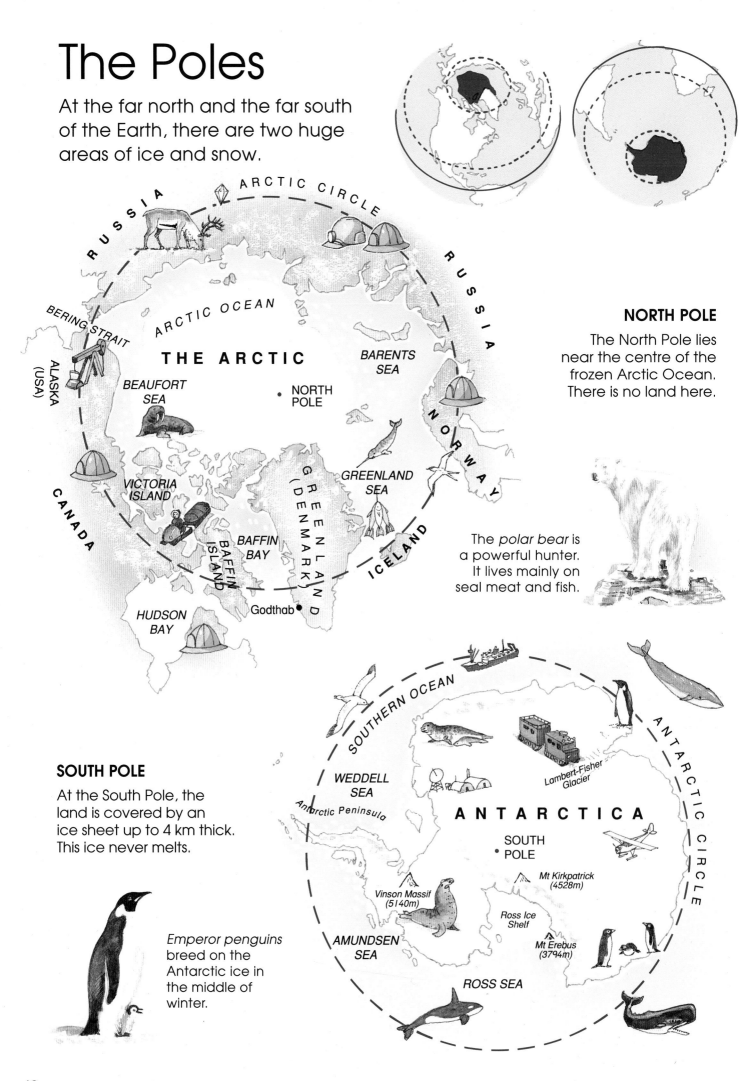

RUSSIA

ARCTIC CIRCLE

RUSSIA

BERING STRAIT

ALASKA (USA)

ARCTIC OCEAN

THE ARCTIC

BEAUFORT SEA

NORTH POLE

BARENTS SEA

NORWAY

VICTORIA ISLAND

CANADA

GREENLAND (DENMARK)

GREENLAND SEA

ICELAND

BAFFIN ISLAND

BAFFIN BAY

HUDSON BAY

Godthab

NORTH POLE

The North Pole lies near the centre of the frozen Arctic Ocean. There is no land here.

The *polar bear* is a powerful hunter. It lives mainly on seal meat and fish.

SOUTH POLE

At the South Pole, the land is covered by an ice sheet up to 4 km thick. This ice never melts.

Emperor penguins breed on the Antarctic ice in the middle of winter.

SOUTHERN OCEAN

WEDDELL SEA

Antarctic Peninsula

ANTARCTICA

Lambert-Fisher Glacier

SOUTH POLE

ANTARCTIC CIRCLE

Mt Kirkpatrick (4528m)

Vinson Massif (5140m)

Ross Ice Shelf

Mt Erebus (3794m)

AMUNDSEN SEA

ROSS SEA

Map index

Countries in
CAPITAL LETTERS

Capital cities in
bold type

Continents and oceans
also appear inside the
front cover.

A

Aberdeen 10
Abidjan 26
Abu Dhabi 29
Accra 26
Aconcagua, Mt 25
Addis Ababa 26
Adelaide 38
Aden 29
Aden, Gulf of 29
Adriatic Sea 14,17
Aegean Sea 17
AFGHANISTAN 7,18,28,30
Africa 6–9,16,26–27
Ahmadabad 30
Alabama 23
Alaska 6,19,20,22,40
Alaska, Gulf of 22
ALBANIA 7,17
Alberta 20
Aldan, River 19
ALGERIA 6–7,26
Algiers 26
Alice Springs 38
Alps 14,16
Altai Mountains 19,34
Amazon River 24–25
America, North 6,21–24
America, South 6,24–25
Amman 28
Amsterdam 14
Amundsen Sea 40
Amur, River 19
Anchorage 22
Andaman Islands 31
Andaman Sea 32
Andes 25
ANDORRA 7,16
Angel Falls 24
Angerman, River 12–13
ANGOLA 7,27
Ankara 28
Antananarivo 27
Antarctica 6–9,40
Antarctic Circle 6–9,40
Antarctic Peninsula 40
ANTIGUA & BARBUDA 6
Antwerp 14
Apennines 17
Appalachian Mountains 23
Arabian Sea 29,30
Arafura Sea 33,38
Aral Sea 18
Ararat, Mt 28
Archangel 18
Arctic Circle 6–9,12,
  18–22,40
Arctic Ocean 6,8–9,40
Arctic 40
ARGENTINA 6,25
Arizona 22
Arkansas 23
ARMENIA 7,18,28

Arno, River 17
Ashkhabad 18
Asia 7,9,18–19,28–39
Asuncion 25
Aswan 26
Atacama Desert 25
Athens 17
Atlantic Ocean 6–8,10–11,
  16,21,23,25–27
Atlas Mountains 26
Auckland 37
Australasia 6–7,9,32–33,
  36–39
AUSTRALIA 7,33,38–39
Australian Alps 39
Australian Capital
  Territory 39
AUSTRIA 7,14,17
Avon, River 11
Ayers Rock 38
AZERBAIJAN 7,18,28

B

Baffin Bay 21,40
Baffin Island 21,40
Baghdad 28
BAHAMAS 6,23,24
Baku 18
Balearic Islands 16
BAHRAIN 7,29
Baikal, Lake 19
Balaton, Lake 15
Bali 32
Balkan Mountains 17
Baltic Sea 13,15,18
Bamako 26
Bangalore 31
Bangkok 32
BANGLADESH 7,31
Banks Island 20
BARBADOS 6,24
Barcelona 16
Barents Sea 12,18,40
Bass Strait 39
Beaufort Sea 20,40
Beijing (Peking) 35
Beirut 28
BELARUS 7,15,18
Belfast 10
BELGIUM 6,14,16
Belgrade 17
BELIZE 6,24
Ben Nevis 10
Bengal, Bay of 31
BENIN 6,26
Bergen 13
Bering Sea 19
Bering Strait 19,40
Berlin 14
BERMUDA 6
Berne 14
BHUTAN 7,31
Bilbao 16
Birmingham 11
Biscay, Bay of 16
Biwa, Lake 36
Black Forest 14
Black Sea 15,17,18,28
Blue Nile 26
Bogota 24
BOLIVIA 6,25
Bombay 30
Bonn 14

Bordeaux 16
Borneo 32
BOSNIA AND HERZEGOVINA 17
Boston 23
Bothnia, Gulf of 12–13
BOTSWANA 7,27
Bougainville 33
Brahmaputra, River 31
Brasilia 25
BRAZIL 6,25
Brisbane 39
Bristol 11
British Columbia 20
BRUNEI 7,32
Brussels 14
Bucharest 15
Budapest 15
Buenos Aires 25
BULGARIA 7,15,17
BURKINA FASO 6,26
BURMA see MYANMAR
BURUNDI 7,27

C

Cagliari 16
Cairo 26
Calais 16
Calcutta 31
California 22
CAMBODIA 7,32
Cambridge 11
CAMEROON 7,26
CANADA 6,20–22,40
Canary Islands 26
Canberra 39
Cantabrian Mountains 16
Canterbury Plains 37
Canton see Guangzhou
Cape Horn 25
Cape Town 27
CAPE VERDE ISLANDS 6
Caracas 24
Cardiff 11
Caribbean Sea 24
Carpathian Mountains 15
Carpentaria, Gulf of 38
Carrantuohill 11
Caspian Sea 18,28
Caucasus Mountains 18
Cayenne 24
CAYMAN ISLANDS 6
Celebes 32
Celebes Sea 32
CENTRAL AFRICAN
  REPUBLIC 7,26
CHAD 7,26
Channel Islands 11
Charlottetown 21
Chicago 23
CHILE 6,25
CHINA 7,18,31,32,34–35
Chongqing (Chungking) 35
Christchurch 37
Chungking see Chongqing
Churchill River 20
Citlaltepetl, Mt 24
Clyde, River 10
Cologne 14
COLOMBIA 6,24
Colombo 31
Colorado 22
Colorado River 22
Communism, Mt 18

CANADA

VENEZUELA

UNITED STATES
OF AMERICA

COLOMBIA

MEXICO

ECUADOR

BAHAMAS

PERU

CUBA

GUYANA

TRINIDAD &
TOBAGO

BRAZIL

BARBADOS

BOLIVIA

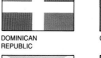
DOMINICAN
REPUBLIC

CHILE

JAMAICA

PARAGUAY

GUATEMALA

ARGENTINA

EL SALVADOR

URUGUAY

NICARAGUA

ICELAND

COSTA RICA

NORWAY

PANAMA

SWEDEN

41

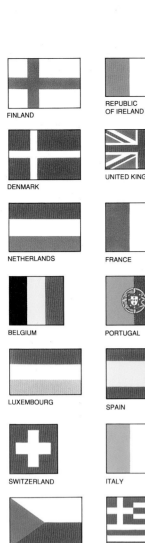
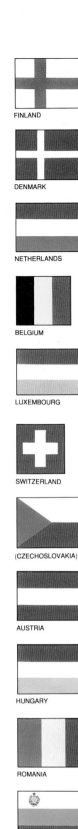

FINLAND

REPUBLIC OF IRELAND

DENMARK

UNITED KINGDOM

NETHERLANDS

FRANCE

BELGIUM

PORTUGAL

LUXEMBOURG

SPAIN

SWITZERLAND

ITALY

(CZECHOSLOVAKIA)

GREECE

AUSTRIA

MALTA

HUNGARY

CYPRUS

ROMANIA

MOROCCO

BULGARIA

ALGERIA

ALBANIA

TUNISIA

POLAND

LIBYA

GERMANY

EGYPT

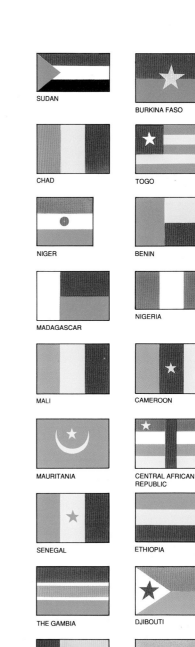

SUDAN
BURKINA FASO
CHAD
TOGO
NIGER
BENIN
MADAGASCAR
NIGERIA
MALI
CAMEROON
MAURITANIA
CENTRAL AFRICAN REPUBLIC
SENEGAL
ETHIOPIA
THE GAMBIA
DJIBOUTI
GUINEA-BISSAU
SOMALIA

GUINEA
UGANDA

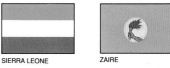

SIERRA LEONE
ZAIRE

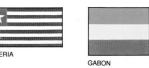

LIBERIA
GABON

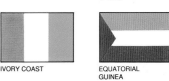

IVORY COAST
EQUATORIAL GUINEA

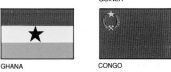

GHANA
CONGO

RWANDA

BURUNDI

KENYA

TANZANIA

ANGOLA

ZAMBIA

MALAWI

MOZAMBIQUE

ZIMBABWE

NAMIBIA

BOTSWANA

SWAZILAND

LESOTHO

MAURITIUS

SEYCHELLES

SOUTH AFRICA

SRI LANKA

TURKEY

LEBANON

ISRAEL

SYRIA

JORDAN

IRAQ

IRAN

SAUDI ARABIA

KUWAIT

YEMEN

OMAN

Index of special features

BAHRAIN

VIETNAM

QATAR

CAMBODIA

UNITED ARAB EMIRATES

MALAYSIA

AFGHANISTAN

BRUNEI

PAKISTAN

SINGAPORE

INDIA

NORTH KOREA

BANGLADESH

SOUTH KOREA

BHUTAN

TAIWAN

MYANMAR (BURMA)

JAPAN

CHINA

PHILIPPINES

MONGOLIA

INDONESIA

PAPUA NEW GUINEA

THAILAND

AUSTRALIA

LAOS

NEW ZEALAND